BECAUSE
YOU DIED

POETRY AND PROSE OF
THE FIRST WORLD WAR
AND AFTER

VERA BRITTAIN

Edited with an introduction by
MARK BOSTRIDGE

virago

VIRAGO

First published in Great Britain in 2008 by Virago Press

Copyright © Poetry and Prose
The Literary Executors of the Vera Brittain Estate 1970
Copyright © Introduction and Selection Mark Bostridge 2008

A CIP catalogue record for this book
is available from the British Library.

ISBN 978-1-84408-413-5
2142555
Typeset in Goudy by M Rules
Printed and bound in Great Britain by
Clays Ltd, St Ives plc

Papers used by Virago are natural, renewable and recyclable
products, made from wood grown in sustainable forests and certified
in accordance with the rules of the Forest Stewardship Council.

Mixed Sources
Product group from well-managed
forests and other controlled sources
www.fsc.org Cert no. SGS-COC-004081
© 1996 Forest Stewardship Council

Virago Press
An imprint of
Little, Brown Book Group
100 Victoria Embankment
London EC4Y 0DY

An Hachette Livre UK Company
www.hachettelivre.co.uk

www.virago.co.uk

For Tim and Rebecca
chronologically

CONTENTS

Introduction xiii

PART ONE

POETRY

August 1914 3

St Pancras Station, August 1915 5

To a Fallen Idol 6

To Monseigneur 9

The Only Son 11

Perhaps— 12

A Military Hospital 15

Looking Westward 17

Then and Now 19

May Morning 20

The Two Travellers 23

The Sisters Buried at Lemnos 24

In Memoriam: G.R.Y.T. 26

A Parting Word 29

The Troop-Train 30

Sic Transit— 33

To Them 34

Oxford Revisited 37

The German Ward 38

Roundel 41

To My Ward-Sister 43

To Another Sister 44

War 47

'Vengeance is Mine' 49

The Last Post 51

To My Brother 52

That Which Remaineth 55

The Aspirant 56

Reinstated 59

A Farewell 61

Hospital Sanctuary 62

To a VC 65

Requiem 67

After Three Years 69

Flotsam of War 70

Epitaph for Edward 73

Epitaph on My Days in Hospital 75

To Any Victim of Circumstances 76

In a Summerhouse 79

The End 80

The New Stoicism 82

Boar's Hill, October 1919 85

The Lament of the Demobilised 87

Anniversaries 89

The Superfluous Woman 91

The Unseen Undergraduates 93

We Shall Come No More 94

The War Generation: Ave 96

The War Generation: Vale 99

PART TWO

PROSE

24th General Hospital,
British Expeditionary Force, France 103

The Asiago Plateau 109

Our Backs to the Wall. A Memory of the War 113

Their Name Liveth. Forgetting Women's War-Work 119

The Real VAD. From Fancy Back to Fact 125

A Poppy For Her Cot. Some Armistice Reflections 132

Re-Encounter 137

While We Remember. The Purpose of Armistice Day ... 143

Diary Extract. Summer 1933 147

Illusion on the Somme 174

What Nursing Taught Me 180

War Service in Perspective 186

Notes 210

Because you died, I shall not rest again

Vera Brittain (front row, centre) with her parents Arthur (front row, right) and Edith (back row, right), and Buxton friend Maurice Ellinger (front row, left). Derbyshire, *circa* 1912

INTRODUCTION

As a young girl growing up in Macclesfield and Buxton, Vera Brittain (1893–1970) dreamed of becoming a published writer. Her early literary efforts were precocious. A series of 'novels', written between the ages of seven and eleven on waste-cuts from her father's paper mill, centred on a family of five daughters who lived in Macclesfield. Like the Victorian melodramas on which she had been raised, these childhood fictions were filled with violent deaths and tearful notions of self-sacrifice. By 1905, when Vera went to her first school, The Grange at Buxton in Derbyshire, she was writing poetry. The death of Edward VII in the summer of 1910, when she was a sixteen-year-old pupil at St Monica's School in Kingswood, Surrey, provided her with the occasion for a commemorative tribute in verse: 'The noble deeds of England's king survive his passing knell, / And still give comfort to the hearts of those who loved him well.'

Preparing to leave St Monica's at the end of 1911, to begin her rite of passage as a provincial debutante, Vera Brittain's image of herself as a writer was as strong as ever. In one of her final school essays, she imagined her ideal room as a plain, book-lined study: a stark contrast to the stuffy, over-furnished surroundings of her Buxton home, where books were in distinctly short supply. Back in Derbyshire, it did not take long for the round of social duties expected of a daughter at home to pall. Within a year Vera was longing to escape from the tedium of this life of calls and entertaining, of local balls and bridge parties, and in 1913 she took her first steps towards becoming an undergraduate at Oxford University. In the spring of 1914 she won an exhibition to Somerville College, academically the most rigorous of Oxford's three women's colleges; and that summer, as the European crisis toppled over into war, she overcame the final hurdle in gaining admission to the University itself by passing the Oxford Senior Local Examination. In October 1914, Vera went up to Somerville to study for a degree in English. Half of Oxford's male undergraduates had already deserted their colleges to enlist. Vera's own brother Edward, her junior by almost two years, forfeited his place at university to apply for a commission in the army, along with his Uppingham schoolfriends Roland Leighton and Victor Richardson.

Against this background of war, Oxford, and the intellectual life it represented, began to appear increasingly irrelevant to Vera herself. Her growing relationship with Roland Leighton, who departed for the Front at the end of March 1915, encouraged Vera to take the decision that she hoped might eventually bring her as close to the dangers of the conflict as it was possible for a woman to be. In the summer of 1915 she obtained permission to interrupt her studies in order to start work as a probationary Voluntary Aid Detachment (VAD) nurse at Buxton's dome-capped Devonshire Hospital. The VAD scheme had been established in 1909, under the auspices of the British Red Cross

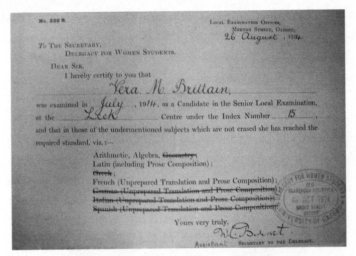

Vera passed the Oxford Senior just as war was breaking out

and the St John Ambulance Association, to assist the profes-
sional military nursing service in the event of a national
emergency. Within months of the outbreak of war the VAD
organisation had begun to expand, and in 1916, by which time
the devastating effects of trench warfare were evident, it had
eighty thousand members under contract, including cooks, ward
maids and motor drivers, as well as nursing auxiliaries. VAD
nurses were almost exclusively drawn from middle- and upper-
class backgrounds, a stereotype to which Vera Brittain clearly
conformed. Before the end of 1915 she had transferred to her first
military hospital, the 1st London General, in Camberwell, and in
September of the following year she accepted a foreign posting to
Malta. On the third anniversary of the outbreak of war, 4 August

1917, Vera arrived at the 24 General at Etaples in France, a base hospital close to the Western Front. She was experiencing 'real Active Service conditions at last'.

Vera at home at Melrose, Buxton, *circa* 1913

The war cut across Vera Brittain's ambitions, but it also forged her identity as a writer. In her diary, and in letters to four male contemporaries at the Front, as well as in drafts of unfinished novels and, of course, in her eventual memoir, *Testament of Youth*, she charted a tragic course of events as 'history's greatest disaster' shaped and altered her personal destiny for ever.

Poetry, however, was the form of Vera Brittain's earliest published observations about the First World War. In late August 1918, as the war was coming to an end with fierce fighting on the Western Front, a slim volume of her *Verses of a V.A.D.*, the first of the twenty-nine books that Vera was to publish in her fifty-year writing career, made its appearance on a market already saturated with war poetry. *Mr Punch's History of the Great War*, also published that summer, remarked upon the way in which the war 'has not only stimulated the composition, but the perusal of poetry among women'. Vera later recalled that, throughout the war, poetry was the only literature she had been able to read for comfort, 'and the only kind that I ever attempted to write'. While on active service, she and Edward Brittain – who, out in France with the 11th Sherwood Foresters, found that 'poetry counteracts the deadening influence a good deal' – often exchanged books of verse. Thomas Hardy's *Selected Poems* from 1916, Gilbert Frankau's *The City of Fear* (1918), and Robert Nichols's best-selling collection of 1917, *Ardours and Endurances*, in which the poet suffers the deaths in action of his two closest friends, leaving him with 'an irredeemable loneliness', were among those they read, and it was to Edward that Vera often turned for criticism and comment on her own attempts.

A foreword to *Verses of a V.A.D.* by Marie Connor Leighton, who before the war had been a successful author of sensational melodramas for the Northcliffe Press, made a special plea on the book's behalf. She asked for 'considerateness and tender sympathy' from critics judging work that had been produced 'in almost breathless intervals of severe and devoted duty', and reminded them that the circumstances of nursing in a military hospital made it difficult 'to achieve any literary ornamentation and least of all that particular kind of simpleness which is the highest form of art'. Mrs Leighton had a personal interest of her own to declare: where pain was expressed in the poems, she admitted, 'it has almost always been my pain as well as the author's'. She was referring to the death of her son, mortally wounded in France in December 1915, when he was shot by a German sniper as he inspected the barbed wire in front of a trench. *Verses of a V.A.D.* was dedicated to the memory of Roland Leighton, 'Lieutenant, Worcestershire Regiment', who had 'Died of Wounds near Hébuterne' on 23 December 1915. Beneath the dedication were lines from Roland's poem 'Good-bye', in which he had written prophetically that 'We two shall live our passionate poem through / On God's serene to-morrow.'

Vera Brittain and Roland Leighton had become engaged, for three years or the duration of the war, at the end of August 1915 while he was home on a short leave. They had first been attracted to each other in April 1914, when Roland came to stay with Edward in Buxton during the school holidays. In July, just weeks before the outbreak of war, the intimacy between Vera and Roland had grown at the Uppingham School Speech Day, later described by Vera as 'the one perfect summer idyll that I ever experienced', where Roland had broken the Uppingham record for school prizes by winning the seven main ones. As they parted after spending three days together, she wrote in her diary that 'He seems even in a short acquaintance to share both my faults and my talents and my ideas in a way that I have never found anyone else to yet.' By December of that year, when they met in London at the end of Vera's first term at Somerville, they were exchanging photographs and their relationship had moved closer to love.

'In this time of tragedy there can be no postponement.' The war intensified Vera and Roland's relationship, and accelerated its pace, especially after Roland manoeuvred a transfer to the 7th Worcestershire Regiment and was posted to Ploegsteert Wood ('Plug Street Wood') a few miles from the Franco-Belgian border. In all they were to meet on only seven occasions, for a total of seventeen days, and just three of them after they had fallen in love. But while the enforced separations of war made a conventional romance impossible, their knowledge of one another grew through the letters they exchanged, even though at times it seemed to both of them that the object of their love was becoming increasingly a figure of their imagination.

Poetry was initially another bond between them. Part of Roland's attraction was that he was the son of two writers – his father, Robert Leighton, published stories for boys and had been the first literary editor of the *Daily Mail* – and that he shared Vera's passion for literature, together with her literary ambitions. For Roland was himself a young poet of promise, who continued to write poetry in the long and tedious stretches of time he spent in trenches or in billets behind the lines, waiting for the chance to prove himself in a major action or great push, which never came. In April 1915, soon after arriving at the Front, Roland wrote a letter to Vera from Ploegsteert Wood, enclosing some violets from the top of his dug-out, which he said he had picked for her. Four months later, during what turned out to be his final leave, Roland allowed Vera to read the 'Villanelle' ('Violets from Plug Street') he had been inspired to write by the memory of picking the flowers.

> I handed it back to him without criticism. I could not have made any; the union of brilliance of intellect with personal love closed my lips quite effectually. Not until after I had parted from him & he sent me the poem enclosed in a letter did I dare to say how perfect I thought this small literary gem of his. I only said 'Why didn't you send me this at the same time as the violets?' 'Oh I don't know,' he said. 'It wasn't finished for one thing.'

Rupert Brooke's war sonnets, 1914, with their spirit of patriotic idealism, had a profound effect on Vera Brittain. In May 1915, only a few weeks after Brooke's death in the Aegean, she had been one of a small group of undergraduates who listened to the sonnets being read aloud by Somerville's English tutor, Helen Darbishire. Vera found them 'so sad that I could scarcely keep back tears'. She copied out four of the sonnets and sent them to Roland with her next letter. The following month she read them to Edward while he was on leave, and noted that they 'seemed to stir him deeply'. Throughout the rest of the war, Vera would quote freely from Brooke in her diary and letters, and, as for so many of her generation, Brooke's sonnets became a source of strength and courage. For Roland, though, forced to face the disparity between the glamorous vision of war evoked by a patriotic poet and the grim reality of twentieth-century warfare experienced in the trenches, admiration for Rupert Brooke was more difficult to sustain. Writing to Vera in September 1915, a month after she had sent him a copy of 1914, Roland made a powerful and damning rejection of Brooke-style rhetoric. Brooke's name is not mentioned, but the echoes of his third sonnet, 'The Dead' ('These laid the world away; poured out the red / Sweet wine of youth . . .'), quoted with bitter irony, make Roland's intention plain. In the course of superintending the building of some dug-outs, Roland had chanced upon the remains of some dead Germans, 'the fleshless, blackened bones of simple men who poured out their red, sweet wine of youth':

Let him who thinks War is a glorious thing, who loves to roll forth stirring words of exhortation, invoking Honour and Praise and Valour and Love of Country . . . let him but look at a little pile of sodden grey rags that cover half a skull and a shin bone and what might have been Its ribs, or at this skeleton lying on its side . . . and let him realise how grand & glorious a thing it is to have distilled all Youth and Joy and Life into a foetid heap of hideous putrescence. Who is there who has known & seen who can say that Victory is worth the death of even one of these?

A little over three months later, Roland Leighton was dead.

Vera learned of Roland's death at a casualty clearing station in Louvencourt, on 26 December 1915, as she waited at the Grand Hotel in Brighton for him to arrive home on Christmas leave.

The chateau at Louvencourt that formed the casualty clearing station
where Roland Leighton died in December 1915

Her grief was all consuming as she struggled to come to terms with
the fact that his death had been wholly devoid of any glamour, and
had not even appeared to serve any discernible military purpose.
The deaths in quick succession of two other close friends of Vera
and her brother, Victor Richardson and Geoffrey Thurlow, only
reinforced an overwhelming sense of loss. Victor, blinded in April
1917 in an attack on a heavily defended German entrenchment
at Vimy Ridge, died two months later in a London hospital. To
Vera, Victor had 'always been so much of a survival to me of a part
of Roland', and she had returned home from her posting in Malta

to offer him 'a very close & life-long devotion if he would accept it'. Geoffrey, who Vera had befriended in the months following Roland's death, while he was recovering from the shell-shock and slight face wound he had suffered at Ypres, was killed in action on 23 April at Monchy-le-Preux, in an attack on the Scarpe. 'My dear dear Geoffrey!' Vera wrote, commemorating him with another Brooke quotation. 'He leaves a white / Unbroken glory, a gathered radiance, / A width, a shining peace, under the night.'

The need to memorialise these men found an outlet in Vera's verse, and by the autumn of 1917, while she was nursing German prisoners of war at Etaples, Vera had started to make definite plans for a published collection of her poetry. 'I am so glad that you liked the poem on the German ward,' she told her mother. 'Am in the middle of one or two others but they don't get finished very quickly in these days. Should like to publish soon.' Marie Leighton undertook to help her find a publisher. On 24 October 1917, Vera wrote to her mother asking her to 'please send my type-written copy of [my] poems to Mrs Leighton as soon as you can, as she has written to Erskine Macdonald the publisher about bringing them out in a little volume & he wants to see them'. Macdonald was later described by Vera Brittain as 'an experimental publisher', though in other circles he was perceived as a rogue and trickster. Two years earlier, Harold Monro of the Poetry Bookshop had warned Wilfred Owen against publishing with him. 'Erskine Macdonald' was an alias for Galloway Kyle, who had founded the Poetry Society not long before the war to take advantage of the increasing public enthusiasm for poetry. Kyle specialised in making profits out of unsuspecting authors of amateur verse, using the *Poetry Review*, which he had helped establish, to print favourable reviews of the books he published, and being less than upstanding when it came to paying out royalties, only too aware that what his authors cared about most was getting in print. 'Young soldiers, keen to publish before they were killed, and grieving parents, anxious to bring out memorial volumes' were drawn into this racket. In Vera's case, Mrs Leighton's backing together with an offer from Arthur Brittain, Vera's father, to supply 'free of all costs, ten reams of antique printing paper' undoubtedly made the project attractive to Erskine Macdonald Limited. 'Very glad to hear that Erskine Macdonald was so favourable in his criticism', Edward Brittain wrote encouragingly to his sister in February 1918; 'it is certainly rather unusual . . . for him to half-finance a first volume of any sort.'

Nevertheless, Vera soon grew impatient with the lack of progress towards publication and at the beginning of March reported that 'I have written to Erskine Macdonald to jog his unbusinesslike memory'; the following week she asked Edith Brittain if she 'would do something to buck up Erskine Macdonald' as she was 'longing to see the book'. Two months later it had still not appeared, and it was Edward's turn to express his exasperation. 'What is Erskine Macdonald doing with your poems?' he asked Vera. 'I should think it's about time they came out.' By the time *Verses of a V.A.D.* was finally published, at the end of that summer, Edward Brittain had been dead two months, killed in action in the decisive rout of the Austrians at Asiago.

The book attracted a number of favourable reviews. The *Times Literary Supplement* commended Vera on her 'well-finished and exact workmanship', noting that 'she only yields to the need of expressing, simply and clearly and with restraint, an exceptionally poignant personal sorrow for losses in the war'. The *Athenaeum* declared that the poems showed promise, while the *Aberdeen Free Press* was more rapturous in its praise, observing that 'Their want of elaboration adds to their effectiveness and poetical value as a spontaneous outpouring of human feeling aroused by actual circumstances.' The *Yorkshire Observer* struck the only harsh note of criticism. 'Excellent prose,' it commented, 'has often been trans-formed into bad poetry, and were this not a first attempt made in a period of trial, critics might be severe with our VAD.'

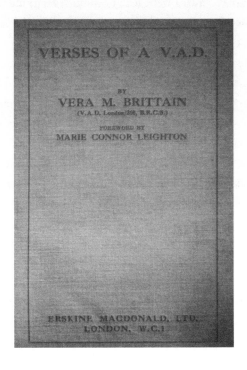

The *Verses* are predominantly elegiac or documentary, and many of them were written in snatched breaks from the hospital routine. In September 1917, for example, Vera Brittain reported that she had been writing a poem about the German ward 'while watching a patient who was rather sick come round from an operation'. Yet she was able to see that the rushed and difficult circumstances of their composition could sometimes contribute a valuable immediacy to the finished work. 'One talks about this VAD work being bad for one's brain,' she wrote to her mother, 'but it is a strange thing, isn't it, that the only poems I have written worth reading have all been written since I went into hospital. The former ones were correct as to verse, metre, etc, but there was no originality about them or life.' Among the hospital poems are tributes to two of the nursing sisters at Etaples with whom Vera Brittain worked – and whom she mildly hero-worshipped – Sister 'Mary' and Faith Moulson, the eccentric ward sister who she would later portray as Hope Milroy in *Testament of Youth*. 'The Sisters Buried at Lemnos' and 'Vengeance is Mine', dedicated to the nurses who were killed in the great air raid on Etaples in May 1918, both reflect Vera Brittain's concern that feats of female heroism should not go unrecorded.

Critics of women's poetry of the First World War during the quarter of a century since the publication of Catherine Reilly's pioneering anthology *Scars Upon My Heart* – a title taken from the opening line of Vera Brittain's 'To My Brother' – have often expressed disappointment about the general quality of these poems, especially for what they perceive as their amateurishness and conventionality. It is not so much that the women poets did not have wartime experiences enough of their own to write about, whether, for example, they were the experience of nursing the wounded and dying, or articulating the searing process of grief and bereavement from the civilian perspective. The problem lies more in the constraints imposed by Victorian and Georgian poetic traditions, and in the dependence of these women on worn-out forms of language and metre, deeply imbued with values that are expressive of a patriotic and essentially masculine ideology.

Although Vera Brittain certainly does not close her eyes to the human cost of war, nor to the 'ruin' and 'individual hell' that, as she writes in 'May Morning', 'only War can bring', there is none of the bitterness, anger or indignation against the war which so strongly characterises her mature reflections in *Testament of Youth*. Perhaps the major explanation for this was the overwhelming need of Vera Brittain, and others like her, to go on sustaining the belief that war was being fought in the service of some great cause, and to keep faith with the men she loved who were facing constant danger. By 1917 she may have been able to admit that her patriotism was a little threadbare, but as a nurse serving close to the front line it would have been virtually impossible for her to have formed a reasoned anti-war point of view. So while in 'The German Ward' she writes of what she had learned from her experience of nursing enemy prisoners ('that human mercy turns alike to friend or foe / When the darkest hour of all is creeping nigh'), these glimmerings of her future pacifism are all but snuffed out by the sentiments of another poem, 'To My Brother', included at a final stage in the preparation of the *Verses*, in which she tries to tell Edward, 'as I could never quite tell him in words or in letters', how much she admired him for his courage and endurance. With its profusion of militaristic imagery, its martial excitement and its hero-worship, 'To My Brother' is essentially a pro-war poem. (It is also, as Simon Featherstone has recently pointed out, a poem about a woman's response to male experience: 'It begins, appropriating the marks of war but subordinating the writer's experience to that of the soldier.') Written four days before Edward Brittain's death in action, and inscribed on the flyleaf of a copy of E.A. Osborn's *The Muse in Arms*, a popular anthology of war poetry that Vera sent out to her brother in Italy, it arrived too late for Edward to read.

Bitterness, arising from a sense of the betrayal of her generation, is the prevailing tone of the poems that Vera Brittain wrote on her return to Oxford, several of which originally appeared in the *Oxford Outlook* and *Oxford Chronicle*, and in the 1919 and 1920 volumes of *Oxford Poetry*. *Because You Died* reprints the war poems from Vera Brittain's second volume of verse, *Poems of the War and After*, published in 1934 in the wake of *Testament of Youth*'s success. This included two of Vera Brittain's most famous and heartfelt poems that express her post-war desolation, 'The Lament of the Demobilised' and 'The Superfluous Woman'.

Inevitably, that spirit of desolation would be at its most intense in the years immediately following the end of the war. Vera's six-month contract at Queen Alexandra's Hospital, Millbank, the second of the two civilian hospitals at which she had nursed after her return from France, came to an end at the beginning of April 1919. At the end of that month she went back to Somerville, where she decided to read history in place of her original degree choice, English, in an attempt to understand the course of events that had culminated in world war. She didn't require the two minutes' silence on Armistice

Day in which to think of the dead, she was to tell Winifred Holtby, the fellow undergraduate she had met on her return to Oxford, whose friendship offered her a lifeline from despair. 'They're with me always; it's like putting two minutes aside in which to breathe.'

Like others who mourned their war dead, Vera Brittain showed an interest, though only fleetingly, in spiritualism. The simple desire to converse with the dead was, not surprisingly, one shared by many people, both during the 1914–18 war and in the aftermath of the years of conflict. This spiritualist revival in Britain is best exemplified by the runaway success of Oliver Lodge's book *Raymond*, which went through a dozen printings between 1916 and 1919 before it was republished in abridged form in 1922. Lodge's son Raymond had been killed on the Ypres Salient in 1915 and Lodge, a distinguished physicist, and his wife subsequently attended seances led by a celebrated medium, through whom they believed they were able to communicate with their dead son. Lodge's book included a memoir of Raymond in the form of his letters home and a record of his parents' communications with him, together with chapters devoted to a philosophical consideration of psychical phenomena.

Vera Brittain attended seances at the behest of her Somerville friend Nina Ruffer. In the summer of 1919 Vera reported to her mother that 'Miss Ruffer . . . is rather a psychic person & immensely interested in spiritualism & we have had various attempts at automatic writing with interesting results . . . Someone calling himself "Edward" often comes & we have had one or two interesting conversations . . . "Roland" has also been but only once & that was yesterday.' She went on to report the details of a conversation with 'Edward'.

> . . . Are you happy? (Vera asking questions)
> No.
> Why not?
> Because you miss me.
> Does that make you unhappy?
> Yes, I want you to be happy.
> How does it affect you if I am unhappy?
> It keeps me back . . .

This dabbling in the spiritual world ended abruptly with the sudden death, later that summer, of Nina Ruffer, from an attack of pneumonia.

The prose pieces chosen for this collection span half a century, from Vera Brittain's report in 1917 for her old school magazine, describing the experience of nursing German prisoners of war in France, to her mature reflections on her war service, written within a few years of her death. They complement the subject matter of the poetry as well as illustrating several interrelated strands of Vera Brittain's life and work in the twenties and early thirties, as she struggled to establish her reputation as a writer. One of these was her pressing need to erect a literary memorial to Roland, Edward, Victor and Geoffrey, and, in so doing, to exorcise her own 'brutal, poignant, insistent memories' of the past; another was to ensure that the female dimension to the war, always under threat of being sidelined, was not forgotten. Perhaps the most urgent, in the light of the fragile international situation, was her recognition that another generation had to be warned against the danger of succumbing to the temptations offered by the glorification of war. In 1933, after completing *Testament of Youth*, Vera Brittain visited the battlefields of the Somme. Standing before the recently unveiled Memorial to the Missing of the Somme at Thiepval, she contemplated the way in which the neatly mown lawns and peaceful cemeteries, filled with flowers, helped to create the illusion that 'war is a glorious thing because so much of its aftermath can be rendered lovely and dignified'. In early 1937 she would embrace the pacifism that was to dominate the rest of her life.

Vera at her home, 19 Glebe Place, Chelsea, around the time of the publication of *Testament of Youth*, 1933

Much of this prose also reflects the fact that, for Vera Brittain, the experience of nursing in France in 1917–18, at the 24 General at Etaples, represented the climax of her wartime service. Before the end of 1917 the German army had made a significant attack near Cambrai, resulting in a flood of casualties to Vera's hospital; in the March of the following year, the 24 General was again overwhelmed with dying and wounded during the German spring offensive. 'Well Malta was an interesting experience of the world,' Vera wrote in a letter home, 'but *this* is War. There is a great coming & going all day long – men marching from one place "somewhere" in France to another, ambulances, transports etc passing all the time . . . Everything of war that one can imagine is here, except actual fighting, & one can even hear the distant rumble of that at times.'

Etaples was the British army's largest-ever hospital and reinforcement camp, providing not only hospitals but also prisons, stores, railway yards and port facilities, as well as infantry depots through which more than a million officers and men had passed by September 1917, for regrouping and training on their way to the Front. The first hospital at Etaples had opened in the spring of 1915. Two-and-a-half years later there were nearly twenty military hospitals, housed in timber buildings and under canvas, the largest containing up to three thousand patients at any one time. This vast encampment has been described as like a large town or small city, several thousand of whose population changed on a daily basis. (During August 1917, Vera's first month at Etaples, almost three thousand officers, and more than thirty thousand other ranks, arrived there, while 2432 officers and 51,707 other ranks were dispatched to the Front from various depots.) Etaples was also the scene, in September 1917, of the British Army's only serious mutiny of the war. On 9 September Colonel R.H. Penton, commanding the 24 General Hospital, recorded a 'Disturbance in Reinforcement Camp between Military Police and Troops', which escalated over succeeding days with violent crowds on the Three Arch Bridge and in the town throwing stones and creating further disturbances. Vera's recollection of 'the Battle of Eetapps' was understandably hazy as she, like other nursing and medical staff, was confined to her hospital for the entire period of the outbreak.

The 24 General admitted the bulk of the sick and wounded of the German prisoners of war, both officers and men, and it was to this ward that Vera was assigned for a period of about five weeks on her arrival at Etaples, on 4 August. The German ward played a pivotal role over the course of the next twenty years, in the development of first Vera's internationalism and subsequently her pacifism. Her experience there was to provide her with the fundamental realisation that a dying man has no nationality. It comes, therefore, as something of a surprise to discover in examining the records kept by the commanding officer of the 24 General that, contrary to the accounts in Vera's letters home, which describe the majority of her German patients as 'more or less dying', the statistics for the period show a very low mortality rate – in fact as low as 2 per cent among the prisoner-patients. How is one to account for this discrepancy?

There is little doubt that after the relative quiescence of her time as a VAD in Malta, where Vera rarely encountered patients who were seriously ill, the 'Active Service conditions' of the 24 General must have offered a marked, even a welcome, contrast; nor can it be disputed that in all the pressure and excitement she initially exaggerated the plight of her German patients. When she came to write her account of Etaples in *Testament of Youth*, more than a decade later, this earlier exaggeration was allowed to colour the substance and tone of her description of the German ward. It should be added in extenuation that the part of the book devoted to her period as a VAD in France does not possess the reliability of precise chronology and detail of earlier chapters, for the simple reason that Vera had ceased to keep a diary on her return from Malta in April 1917, and had only some letters to her mother, and a few rushed notes to Edward, on which to base her account. Equally, though, there is no escaping the fact that the chilling power of her largely fictional recollection of German prisoners dying in vast numbers fits appropriately with the overarching anti-war theme of *Testament of Youth*.

Throughout the course of the 1960s, as the First World War began to make an impact on popular history, the conflict was still viewed overwhelmingly as a masculine experience. This lack of interest in the wartime role of women was starkly demonstrated in 1964 – the fiftieth anniversary of the outbreak of war – when BBC Television's landmark documentary series, *The Great War*, devoted only minutes of its total running time of over seventeen hours to recounting women's experiences. By 1968, when the BBC arranged to film a *Yesterday's Witness* interview with Vera Brittain, it was in a sense too late: the arterial sclerosis that would kill her two years later was already so advanced that her memory of the distant past had begun seriously to erode.

That same year, however, *Promise of Greatness*, a collection of essays edited by George A. Panichas of the University of Maryland, was published to commemorate the fiftieth anniversary of the Armistice. The male writers chosen for the volume included Edmund Blunden, Gerald Brenan, Robert Graves, L.P. Hartley, John Lehmann, Alec Waugh, R.H. Mottram and R.C. Sherriff, but Vera was the only woman. 'An incisive as well as an evocative essay', as Panichas called it, 'War Service in Perspective' was one of her last substantial pieces of writing and it is reprinted here to close this collection of Vera Brittain's First World War poetry and prose.

Looking back, Vera Brittain recalled the confidence of her own generation, growing to maturity just before the outbreak of war, in the idea that what mattered were not public issues 'but the absorbing incidents of our private lives – our careers, ambitions, friendships, and love affairs'. Four years of conflict were enough to change that perception – at least in her own mind. The War left her with an abiding belief, that public issues and private lives 'had become bewilderingly inseparable'. It was no longer possible to believe – as she had been brought up to believe – that human happiness was normal and disaster exceptional, or that one could go through one's life unaffected by the influence of world events.

Vera Brittain died on 29 March 1970. Her ashes were scattered later that year on her brother's grave, in the small cemetery at Granezza on the Asiago Plateau.

*

My thanks to Shirley Williams, Vera Brittain's daughter, to David Leighton, Roland Leighton's nephew, and to Shiona Robotham, Victor Richardson's niece, for their kindness and support over the years. I am grateful to Dominic Hibberd, doyen of critics and anthologists of First World War poetry, for some sage advice; to Margaret Howatson for identifying a quotation from Heraclitus; and to Kate Lindsay for her help in obtaining digital images of some of the photographs and holographs.

At McMaster University in Hamilton, Ontario, which owns Vera Brittain's archive, I am greatly indebted to Carl Spadoni, Head of Special Collections, for his considerable kindness, hospitality and assistance during my visit in 2007. My thanks also to Renu Barrett and Adele Petrovic for all the help they provided in locating material in the collection.

At Virago, I have benefited enormously from the interest and professionalism of Lennie Goodings. My thanks to Linda Silverman, who has patiently traced and obtained photographs from various public collections, and to Zoë Gullen, Susan de Soissons, Marie Hrynczak and Rachael Ludbrook.

Because You Died is published as a book of remembrance to commemorate the ninetieth anniversary of the Armistice, which ended the First World War in November 1918. Its publication also marks the thirtieth anniversary of Virago's republication of *Testament of Youth*, which, as well as helping to establish Virago's reputation, pushed Vera Brittain's famous autobiography to the top of the bestseller charts for the second time in almost half a century. The following year, BBC Television produced its classic adaptation of the book, starring Cheryl Campbell, with a script by Elaine Morgan, which has retained its place as one of the outstanding achievements in television drama of the golden age of British public service broadcasting.

I should like to end on a note of personal remembrance. My maternal grandmother, who died in 1989, in her hundredth year, was one of hundreds of thousands of women in Britain who suffered bereavement as a result of the First World War. On the first day of the Battle of the Somme, in July 1916, her first husband – not my grandfather – was blown to pieces by an exploding shell; in mid-September, as fighting still raged on the Somme, her only brother, just eighteen, was also killed. Today he is buried in Caterpillar Valley Cemetery at Longueval, the long and winding valley that rises eastwards to high ground at Guillemont. My grandmother never spoke much about the tragedies that had unexpectedly transformed her existence, but it must have cost her a great deal to rebuild her life.

Mark Bostridge
April 2008

PART ONE
POETRY

Devonshire Hospital, Buxton

The Devonshire Hospital where Vera began her wartime nursing

Vera with tennis partners, summer 1914

AUGUST 1914

God said, 'Men have forgotten Me;
   The souls that sleep shall wake again,
And blinded eyes must learn to see.'

So since redemption comes through pain
   He smote the earth with chastening rod,
And brought Destruction's lurid reign;

But where His desolation trod
   The people in their agony
Despairing cried, 'There is no God.'

Roland Leighton

ST PANCRAS STATION, AUGUST 1915

One long, sweet kiss pressed close upon my lips,
    One moment's rest on your swift-beating heart,
And all was over, for the hour had come
            For us to part.

A sudden forward motion of the train,
    The world grown dark although the sun still shone,
One last blurred look through aching tear-dimmed eyes—
            And you were gone.

TO A FALLEN IDOL

O you who sought to rend the stars from Heaven
    But rent instead your too-ambitious heart,
Know that with those to whom Love's joy is given
    You have not, nor can ever have, a part.

A nation's loyalty might have been your glory,
    And men have blessed your name from shore
        to shore,
But you have set the seal upon your story,
    And must go hence, alone for evermore.

Vera in 1914. She sent this photograph to
Roland Leighton in December of that year

Roland Leighton, 1915

TO MONSEIGNEUR

(R.A.L., LIEUTENANT, WORCESTERS)

None shall dispute Your kingship, nor declare
    Another could have held the place You hold,
    For though he brought me finer gifts than
        gold,
And laid before my feet his heart made bare
Of all but love for me, and sighed despair
    If I but feigned my favours to withhold,
    And would repudiate as sadly cold
The proud and lofty manner that You wear,

He would not be my pure and stainless knight
    Of heart without reproach or hint of fear,
Who walks unscathed amid War's sordid ways
By base desire or bloodshed's grim delight,
    But ever holds his hero's honour dear—
Roland of Roncesvalles in modern days.

Edward Brittain with Vera, *circa* 1899

THE ONLY SON

The storm beats loud, and you are far away,
      The night is wild,
On distant fields of battle breaks the day,
      My little child?

I sought to shield you from the least of ills
      In bygone years,
I soothed with dreams of manhood's far-off hills
      Your baby fears,

But could not save you from the shock of strife;
      With radiant eyes
You seized the sword and in the path of Life
      You sought your prize.

The tempests rage, but you are fast asleep;
      Though winds be wild
They cannot break your endless slumbers deep,
      My little child.

PERHAPS—

(TO R.A.L. DIED OF WOUNDS IN FRANCE,
DECEMBER 23RD, 1915)

Perhaps some day the sun will shine again,
    And I shall see that still the skies are blue,
And feel once more I do not live in vain,
    Although bereft of You.

Perhaps the golden meadows at my feet
    Will make the sunny hours of Spring seem gay,
And I shall find the white May blossoms sweet,
    Though You have passed away.

Perhaps the summer woods will shimmer bright,
    And crimson roses once again be fair,
And autumn harvest fields a rich delight,
    Although You are not there.

Perhaps some day I shall not shrink in pain
    To see the passing of the dying year,
And listen to the Christmas songs again
    Although You cannot hear.

But, though kind Time may many joys renew,
    There is one greatest joy I shall not know
Again, because my heart for loss of You
    Was broken, long ago.

Roland's grave at Louvencourt

A group of Vera's patients at Camberwell, 1916

A MILITARY HOSPITAL

A mass of human wreckage, drifting in
　　Borne on a blood-red tide,
Some never more to brave the stormy sea
　　Laid reverently aside,
And some with love restored to sail again
　　For regions far and wide.

Edward Brittain, 1915

LOOKING WESTWARD

'For a while the quiet body
Lies with feet toward the Morn.'
HYMN 499, A. & M.

When I am dead, lay me not looking East,
    But towards the verge where daylight sinks to rest,
For my Beloved, who fell in War's dark year,
    Lies in a foreign meadow, facing West.

He does not see the Heavens flushed with dawn,
    But flaming through the sunset's dying gleam;
He is not dazzled by the Morning Star,
    But Hesper soothes him with her gentle beam.

He faces not the guns he thrilled to hear,
    Nor sees the skyline red with fires of Hell;
He looks for ever towards that dear home land
    He loved, but bade a resolute farewell.

So would I, when my hour has come for sleep,
    Lie watching where the twilight shades grow grey;
Far sooner would I share with him the Night
    Than pass without him to the Splendid Day.

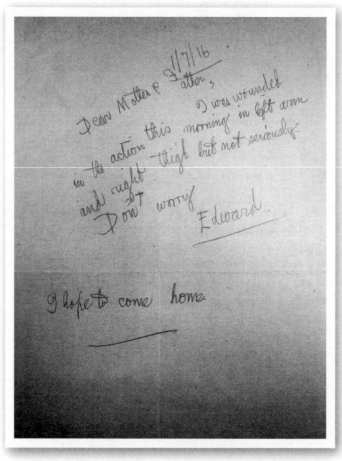

Edward's pencilled note to his parents, informing them that he had
been wounded on the first day of the Battle of the Somme

THEN AND NOW

'πάντα ῥεῖ καὶ οὐδένα μένι'

Once the black pine-trees on the mountain side,
　　The river dancing down the valley blue,
And strange brown grasses swaying with the tide,
　　All spoke to me of you.

But now the sullen streamlet creeping slow,
　　The moaning tree-tops dark above my head,
The weeds where once the grasses used to grow
　　Tell me that you are dead.

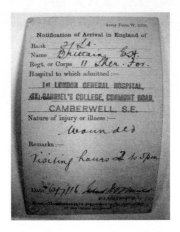

By chance, Edward was sent to the 1st London General
where Vera was nursing as a VAD

MAY MORNING

(*Note* – At Oxford on May 1st a Latin hymn is sung at sunrise by the Magdalen choristers from the top of the tower.)

The rising sun shone warmly on the tower,
    Into the clear pure Heaven the hymn aspired
Piercingly sweet. This was the morning hour
When life awoke with Spring's creative power,
    And the old City's grey to gold was fired.

Silently reverent stood the noisy throng;
    Under the bridge the boats in long array
Lay motionless. The choristers' far song
Faded upon the breeze in echoes long.
    Swiftly I left the bridge and rode away.

Straight to a little wood's green heart I sped,
    Where cowslips grew, beneath whose gold withdrawn
The fragrant earth peeped warm and richly red;
All trace of Winter's chilling touch had fled,
    And song-birds ushered in the year's bright morn.

I had met Love not many days before,
    And as in blissful mood I listening lay
None ever had of joy so full a store.
I thought that Spring must last for evermore,
    For I was young and loved, and it was May.

Now it is May again, and sweetly clear
    Perhaps once more aspires the Latin hymn
From Magdalen tower, but not for me to hear.
I toil far distant, for a darker year
    Shadows the century with menace grim.

I walk in ways where pain and sorrow dwell,
    And ruin such as only War can bring,
Where each lives through his individual hell,
Fraught with remembered horror none can tell,
    And no more is there glory in the Spring.

And I am worn with tears, for he I loved
    Lies cold beneath the stricken sod of France;
Hope has forsaken me, by Death removed.
And Love that seemed so strong and gay has proved
    A poor crushed thing, the toy of cruel Chance.

Often I wonder, as I grieve in vain,
    If when the long, long future years creep slow,
And War and tears alike have ceased to reign,
I ever shall recapture, once again,
    The mood of that May morning, long ago.

Medical personnel at St George's Hospital, Malta where Vera served
as a VAD in 1916–17. She is in the third row,
sixth from the left

THE TWO TRAVELLERS

Beware!
You met two travellers in the town
Who promised you that they would take you down
The valley far away
To some strange carnival this Summer's day.
Take care,
Lest in the crowded street
They hurry past you with forgetting feet,
And leave you standing there.

THE SISTERS BURIED AT LEMNOS

('FIDELIS AD EXTREMUM')

O Golden Isle set in the deep blue Ocean,
    With purple shadows flitting o'er thy crest,
I kneel to thee in reverent devotion
    Of some who on thy bosom lie at rest!

Seldom they enter into song or story;
    Poets praise the soldier's might and deeds of War,
But few exalt the Sisters, and the glory
    Of women dead beneath a distant star.

No armies threatened in that lonely station,
    They fought not fire or steel or ruthless foe,
But heat and hunger, sickness and privation,
    And Winter's deathly chill and blinding snow.

Till mortal frailty could endure no longer
    Disease's ravages and climate's power,
In body weak, but spirit ever stronger,
    Courageously they stayed to meet their hour.

No blazing tribute through the wide world flying,
    No rich reward of sacrifice they craved,

The only meed of their victorious dying
   Lives in the hearts of humble men they saved.

Who when in light the Final Dawn is breaking
   Still faithful, though the world's regard may cease,
Will honour, splendid in triumphant waking,
   The souls of women, lonely here at peace.

O golden Isle with purple shadows falling
   Across thy rocky shore and sapphire sea,
I shall not picture these without recalling
   The Sisters sleeping on the heart of thee!

Vera and fellow VADs in Malta

IN MEMORIAM: G.R.Y.T.

(KILLED IN ACTION, APRIL 23RD, 1917)

I spoke with you but seldom, yet there lay
  Some nameless glamour in your written word,
  And thoughts of you rose often—longings stirred
By dear remembrance of the sad blue-grey
That dwelt within your eyes, the even sway
  Of your young god-like gait, the rarely heard
But frank bright laughter, hallowed by a Day
  That made of Youth Right's offering to the sword.

So now I ponder, since your day is done,
  Ere dawn was past, on all you meant to me,
  And all the more you might have come to be,
And wonder if some state, beyond the sun
  And shadows here, may yet completion see
Of intimacy sweet though scarce begun.

Geoffrey Thurlow

This poem is addressed to Stella Sharp, Vera's old schoolfriend, who served with her as a VAD in London and Malta

A group of VADs at St George's Bay, Malta

A PARTING WORD

(TO A FORTUNATE FRIEND)

If you should be too happy in your days
    And never know an hour of vain regret,
        Do not forget
That still the shadows darken all my ways.

If sunshine sweeter still should light your years,
    And you lose nought of all you dearly prize,
        Turn not your eyes
From my steep track of anguish and of tears.

And if perhaps your love of me is less
    Than I with all my need of you would choose,
        Do not refuse
To love enough to lighten my distress.

And if the future days should parting see
    Of our so different paths that lately met,
        Remember yet
Those days of storm you weathered through with me.

THE TROOP-TRAIN

(FRANCE, 1917)

As we came down from Amiens,
    And they went up the line,
They waved their careless hands to us,
    And cheered the Red Cross sign.

And often I have wondered since,
    Repicturing that train,
How many of those laughing souls
    Came down the line again.

Volunteers in training photographed by Roland Leighton

Victor Richardson

SIC TRANSIT—

(V.R., DIED OF WOUNDS, 2ND LONDON GENERAL HOSPITAL,
CHELSEA, JUNE 9TH, 1917)

I am so tired.
   The dying sun incarnadines the West,
And every window with its gold is fired,
   And all I loved the best
Is gone, and every good that I desired
   Passes away, an idle hopeless quest;
Even the Highest whereto I aspired
   Has vanished with the rest.
I am so tired.

TO THEM

I hear your voices in the whispering trees,
    I see your footprints on each grassy track,
Your laughter echoes gaily down the breeze—
    But you will not come back.

The twilight skies are tender with your smile,
    The stars look down with eyes for which I yearn,
I dream that you are with me all the while—
    But you will not return.

The flowers are gay in gardens that you knew,
    The woods you loved are sweet with summer rain,
The fields you trod are empty now, but you
    Will never come again.

Vera as a VAD in Malta

Having broken her contract to return home from Malta, Vera signed on again in the summer of 1917 and was posted to France

OXFORD REVISITED

There's a gleam of sun on the grey old street
    Where we used to walk in the Oxford days,
And dream that the world lay beneath our feet
    In the dawn of a summer morning.

Now the years have passed, and it's we who lie
    Crushed under the burden of world-wide woe,
But the misty magic will never die
    From the dawn of an Oxford morning.

And the end delays, and perhaps no more
    I shall see the spires of my youth's delight,
But they'll gladden my eyes as in days of yore
    At the dawn of Eternal Morning.

THE GERMAN WARD

('INTER ARMA CARITAS')

When the years of strife are over and my recollection fades
    Of the wards wherein I worked the weeks away,
I shall still see, as a vision rising 'mid the Wartime shades,
    The ward in France where German wounded lay.

I shall see the pallid faces and the half-suspicious eyes,
    I shall hear the bitter groans and laboured breath,
And recall the loud complaining and the weary tedious cries,
    And sights and smells of blood and wounds and death.

I shall see the convoy cases, blanket-covered on the floor,
    And watch the heavy stretcher-work begin,
And the gleam of knives and bottles through the open
        theatre door,
    And the operation patients carried in.

I shall see the Sister standing, with her form of youthful
        grace,
    And the humour and the wisdom of her smile,
And the tale of three years' warfare on her thin expressive
        face—
    The weariness of many a toil-filled while.

I shall think of how I worked for her with nerve and heart
    and mind,
    And marvelled at her courage and her skill,
And how the dying enemy her tenderness would find
    Beneath her scornful energy of will.

And I learnt that human mercy turns alike to friend or foe
    When the darkest hour of all is creeping nigh,
And those who slew our dearest, when their lamps were
    burning low,
    Found help and pity ere they came to die.

So, though much will be forgotten when the sound of War's
    alarms
    And the days of death and strife have passed away,
I shall always see the vision of Love working amidst arms
    In the ward wherein the wounded prisoners lay.

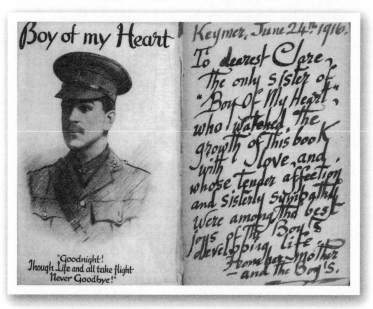

The cover of *Boy of My Heart* (1916), a memoir of Roland by his mother Marie Leighton. The portrait was drawn by Roland's sister Clare, later a distinguished wood-cut artist

ROUNDEL

('DIED OF WOUNDS')

Because you died, I shall not rest again,
But wander ever through the lone world wide,
Seeking the shadow of a dream grown vain
Because you died.

I shall spend brief and idle hours beside
The many lesser loves that still remain,
But find in none my triumph and my pride;

And Disillusion's slow corroding stain
Will creep upon each quest but newly tried,
For every striving now shall nothing gain
Because you died.

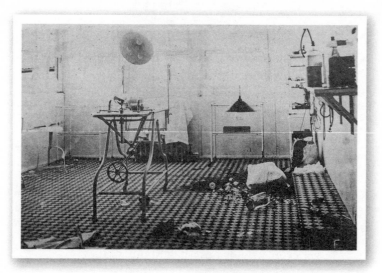

An operating theatre at Etaples

TO MY WARD-SISTER

NIGHT DUTY, DECEMBER 1917

Through the night-watches of our House of Sighs
　　In capable serenity of mind
　　You steadily achieve the tasks designed
With calm, half-smiling, interested eyes;
Though all-unknowing, confidently wise
　　Concerning pain you never felt, you find
Content from uneventful years arise
　　As you toil on, mechanically kind.

So thus far have your smooth days passed, but when
　　The tempest none escape shall cloud your sky,
And Life grow dark around you, through your pain
You'll learn the meaning of your mercy then
　　To those who blessed you as you passed them by,
Nor seek to tread the untroubled road again.

TO ANOTHER SISTER

I knew that you had suffered many things,
   For I could see your eyes would often weep
   Through bitter midnight hours when others sleep;
And in your smile the lurking scorn that springs
   From cruel knowledge of a love, once deep,
Grown gradually cold, until the stings
Pierce mercilessly of a past that clings
   Undying to your lonely path and steep.

So, loved and honoured leader, I would pray
   That hidden future days may hold in store
Some solace for your yearning even yet,
And in some joy to come you may forget
   The burdened toil you will not suffer more
And see the War-time shadows fade away.

A nurse with wounded soldiers at Malta, 1917

FALLEN OFFICERS.

BIOGRAPHIES AND SERVICES.

We have received news of the deaths of the following officers in addition to those officially announced :—

LEIGHTON, LIEUT. R. A., 7th Worcestershire Regt.
SAVORY, CAPT. F. R. E., 1st Shropshire L.I.

The Times would be obliged if relatives of officers who fall in the service of the country would forward *with the intimation of death*, any biographical details in their possession.

LIEUTENANT ROLAND AUBREY LEIGHTON, 7th Worcestershire Regiment, died of wounds in France on December 23, aged 20. The eldest son of Mr. and Mrs. Robert Leighton, of Heather Cliff, Lowestoft, he was educated at Uppingham, where he was a distinguished prizeman, editor of the school magazine, a school præpostor, and a prominent member of the Officers Training Corps. Elected to a classical postmastership at Merton College, Oxford, he had not gone into residence when the war interrupted his scholastic career. He was gazetted to the 4th Norfolk Regiment, but subsequently transferred into the 7th Worcestershire Regiment, and went to the front in April last. During recent weeks he acted as assistant adjutant in the 1st Somersetshire Light Infantry, but returned to his own battalion a fortnight ago. He had been granted leave and was expected home on Christmas morning.

Notice from *The Times*, 28 December 1915

WAR

(THE GREAT GERMAN OFFENSIVE, MARCH–MAY 1918)

A night of storm and thunder crashing by,
 A bitter night of tempest and of rain—
Then calm at dawn beneath a wind-swept sky,
 And broken flowers that will not bloom again.

An age of Death and Agony and Tears,
 A cruel age of woe unguessed before—
Then peace to close the weary storm-wrecked years,
 And broken hearts that bleed for evermore.

The hospitals at Etaples before bombardment in May 1918

'VENGEANCE IS MINE'

(IN MEMORY OF THE SISTERS WHO DIED IN THE GREAT
AIR RAID UPON HOSPITALS AT ETAPLES)

Who shall avenge us for anguish unnamable,
    Rivers of scarlet and crosses of grey,
Terror of night-time and blood-lust untamable,
    Hate without pity where broken we lay?

How could we help them, in agony calling us,
    Those whom we laboured to comfort and save,
How still their moaning, whose hour was befalling us,
    Crushed in a horror more dark than the grave?

Burning of canvas and smashing of wood above—
    Havoc of Mercy's toil—shall He forget
Us that have fallen, Who numbers in gracious love
    Each tiny creature whose life is man's debt?

Will He not hear us, though speech is now failing us—
    Voices too feeble to utter a cry?
Shall they not answer, the foemen assailing us,
    Women who suffer and women who die?

Who shall avenge us for anguish unnamable,
    Rivers of scarlet and crosses of grey,
Terror of night-time and blood-lust untamable,
    Hate without pity where broken we lay?

after

. . . and after

THE LAST POST

The stars are shining bright above the camps,
The bugle calls float skyward, faintly clear;
Over the hill the mist-veiled motor lamps
    Dwindle and disappear.

The notes of day's good-bye arise and blend
    With the low murmurous hum from tree and sod,
And swell into that question at the end
    They ask each night of God—

Whether the dead within the burial ground
    Will ever overthrow their crosses grey,
And rise triumphant from each lowly mound
    To greet the dawning day.

Whether the eyes which battle sealed in sleep
    Will open to reveillé once again,
And forms, once mangled, into rapture leap,
    Forgetful of their pain.

TO MY BROTHER

(IN MEMORY OF JULY 1ST, 1916)

Your battle-wounds are scars upon my heart,
    Received when in that grand and tragic 'show'
You played your part
    Two years ago,

And silver in the summer morning sun
    I see the symbol of your courage glow—
That Cross you won
    Two years ago.

Though now again you watch the shrapnel fly,
    And hear the guns that daily louder grow,
As in July
    Two years ago,

May you endure to lead the Last Advance
    And with your men pursue the flying foe
As once in France
    Two years ago.

To My Brother.
(In memory of July 1st 1916.)

Your battle-wounds are scars upon my heart,
Received when in that grand and tragic "show"
    You played your part
    Two years ago,

And silver in the summer-morning sun
I see the symbol of your courage glow —
    That Cross you won
    Two years ago.

Though now again you watch the shrapnel fly
And hear the guns that daily louder grow
    As in July
    Two years ago,

May you endure to lead the Last Advance,
And with your men pursue the flying foe,
    As once in France
    Two years ago.

——

                              V.M.B.

CAPTAIN
EDWARD H. BRITTAIN M.C.
NOTTS & DERBY REGIMENT
15TH JUNE 1918

AGED 22

Edward Brittain's gravestone at Granezza Cemetery, Asiago

THAT WHICH REMAINETH

(IN MEMORY OF CAPTAIN E.H. BRITTAIN, MC)

Only the thought of a merry smile,
  The wistful dreaming of sad brown eyes—
A brave young warrior, face aglow
  With the light of a lofty enterprise.

Only the hope of a gallant heart,
  The steady strife for a deathless crown,
In Memory's treasures, radiant now
  With the gleam of a goal beyond renown.

Only the tale of a dream fulfilled,
  A strenuous day and a well-fought fight,
A fearless leader who laughed at Death,
  And the fitting end of a gentle knight.

Only a Cross on a mountain side,
  The close of a journey short and rough,
A sword laid down and a stainless shield—
  No more—and yet, is it not enough?

THE ASPIRANT

(A PLEA)

Because I dare to stand outside the gate
   Of that high temple wherein Fame abides
And loudly knock, too eager to await
    Whate'er betides,

May God forgive, since He alone can see
   The joys that others have but I must miss,
For how shall Compensation come to me
    If not through this?

Vera as a VAD

Vera with some of her patients at Malta, 1916

REINSTATED

I had been out of it so long, it seemed;
But back again in uniform at last
I wandered down the busy street and dreamed
Of service even fuller than the past.

And there came by, as merry as could be
Some wounded Tommies in a hired landau,
And one turned round, and waved, and smiled at me
With all the gallant comradeship of War.

The sweet freemasonry of those who serve
Was mine again, a subtle ecstasy;
Life thrilled anew in each awakened nerve
Because a wounded Tommy smiled at me.

Edward before
(above) and after
(right) the Somme,
in which he seemed
to friends to have
aged ten years

A FAREWELL

The twilight shades are falling
   Across the summer sea,
And you have gone your way again
   Without a word to me.

A thrush is gaily singing
   By sweet spring breezes stirred,
But hope lies hidden in your grave
   With that unspoken word.

HOSPITAL SANCTUARY

When you have lost your all in a world's upheaval,
Suffered and prayed, and found your prayers were vain,
When love is dead, and hope has no renewal—
These need you still; come back to them again.

When the sad days bring you the loss of all ambition,
And pride is gone that gave you strength to bear,
When dreams are shattered, and broken is all decision—
Turn you to these, dependent on your care.

They too have fathomed the depths of human anguish,
Seen all that counted flung like chaff away;
The dim abodes of pain wherein they languish
Offer that peace for which at last you pray.

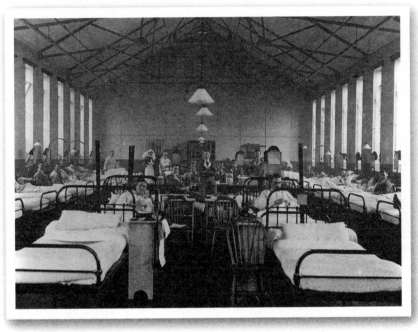

Vera and patients at the 1st London General, Camberwell, *circa* 1916

An old British dug-out, blown out of the rock, on the Asiago Plateau,
photographed by Vera in 1921

TO A VC

Because your feet were stayed upon that road
　　Whereon the others swiftly came and passed,
Because the harvest you and they had sowed
　　You only reaped at last,

'Tis not your valour's meed alone you bear
　　Who stand the hero of a nation's pride;
For on that humble Cross you live to wear
　　Your friends were crucified.

They shared with you the conquest over fear,
　　Sublime self-disregard, decision's power;
But death, relentless, left you lonely here
　　In recognition's hour.

Their sign is yours to carry to the end;
　　The lost reward of gallant hearts as true
As yours they called their leader and their friend
　　Is worn for them by you.

Vera, aged twenty-one, at Camberwell

REQUIEM

Because you've come to the close of a long, long day,
   And shadows lengthen, and night is falling fast,
And all around you the woods are growing grey
   Like the far, dim past;

Because life gave you nothing to keep for long,
   But wrested away from you all she ever bestowed,
Because not one went with you of that loved throng
   To the end of the road,

Be glad you'll rest in the peace of a deep dark night—
   Unless some dawn shall touch the cloud-wrack to gold,
And bring, perhaps, a face with the morning light
   That you loved of old.

Roland Leighton and Victor Richardson outside The Lodge,
Uppingham School, summer 1914

AFTER THREE YEARS

TO R.A.L. (DIED OF WOUNDS, 1915)

What think you now, if you can see me still,
  Of her you loved those endless years ago?
Have I grown commonplace—that greatest ill
To your swift mind—and lost the power to thrill
  You used to know?

Have I so changed, since sorrow set her seal
  On my lost youth, and left me solitary
Amid the dreams of vanished joys, once real,
Or fallen often from that sweet ideal
  You formed of me?

What though no spring shall ever now renew
  The April in my eyes, the wayward will
That could not live through all I have lived through?
I think you love me just the same, if you
  Can see me still.

FLOTSAM OF WAR

We are the flotsam of War
   Washed up by the last high tide,
   The mightier vessels left the shore
For port on the other side.

Vera outside the night quarters at St George's Hospital,
Malta, 1917

EPITAPH FOR EDWARD

Not where the golden sunshine softly smiles
Upon the fields of your lost Happy Isles
You wait for me. Your joyous songs are stilled.
For to the sunset land of Avalon
You and your music and your dreams are gone,
Not here, dear child, not here to be fulfilled.

June 22ⁿᵈ 1918.

Telegram arrives – ..."Captain E. H.
Brittain M.C. killed in action, Italy,
June 15ᵗʰ. "

Blue delphiniums on the dining-room
table.

Etaples before the war

EPITAPH
ON MY DAYS IN HOSPITAL

I found in you a holy place apart,
Sublime endurance, God in man revealed,
Where mending broken bodies slowly healed
My broken heart.

TO ANY VICTIM OF CIRCUMSTANCES

To suffer much and know it unavailing,
    But undismayed pursue your journey still,
To face the barren future without quailing
    And fight your own lost causes with a will,

To weep the long night through, but greet the daytime
    With smiling eyes the brighter for your tears,
To join your happy comrades in their playtime,
    Nor let them bear your burden of lost years,

Here only triumph lies; salvation's earning
    Is wrought through lonely strife and pain concealed.
In fiery conquest over his soul's yearning
    Alone the strength of man can stand revealed.

Vera with a nursing sister, 1917

Vera, *circa* 1913

IN A SUMMERHOUSE

Noon, and a sun-filled garden,
    Scarlet geraniums gay—
Distant far was your glory
    A year ago to-day.

Little we knew of summer,
    Tossed on a flood-tide red.
How could we dream of roses
    Who only saw the dead?

Storm then, and desolation;
    Now August blossoms blow—
Whence came the two together
    In the one world we know?

THE END

When the murmuring voices die
   And the sunlight fades,
When I cannot hear the footsteps hastening by
   Through the gathering shades,

Oh, then I'll remember you!
   On the border-land
I shall live the passionate dream that never came true,
   Led hence by your hand.

And if no to-morrow shall dawn
   To the long night's pain,
What matter? Amid the shadows where dreams are born
   I shall see you again.

The telegram announcing Edward's death in the battle on the Asiago
Plateau, which Vera received in London on 22 June 1918

THE NEW STOICISM

Because you smiled with eyes a little sad
One summer day, and said: 'If I should die,
I would not have you weep, Beloved, nor sigh
For all the dear delights we should have had;
For I would watch you seek amid the stars
Your goal, unweakened by regret or tears,
Nor feel the shadow of my passing mars
Your journey to fulfilment through the years'—
I fling defiance in the cold world's face,
And strive to grow impervious to scorn;
For should I once reveal how much I mourn
The vanished joy no time shall bring, nor space,
You'll seem to whisper: 'Falter not, endure!
And if your heart is breaking, laugh the more!'

Vera, *circa* 1924

Headquarters,

Auberge de Castille,

Malta.

This is to certify that _Miss Vera_

Mary Brittain, _V.A.D.B.R.C.S._

has served in Military Hospitals _since 13.10.15._

& in Malta from 7 $\frac{10}{16}$ to the present date

and is recommended for the Long Service Bar.

a/Matron _M. A. Oakley. T.F.N.S._

St. George's Hospital.

R. Oldroyd

a/ Principal Matron,

Q.A.I.M.N.S.,

Malta.

Date: 18.5.17.

BOAR'S HILL, OCTOBER 1919

Tall slender beech-trees, whispering, touched with fire,
Swaying at even beneath a desolate sky;
Smouldering embers aflame where the clouds hurry by
At the wind's desire.

Dark sombre woodlands, rain-drenched by the scattering
    shower,
Spindle that quivers and drops its dim berries to earth—
Mourning, perhaps, as I mourn here for the dearth
Of a happier hour.

Can you still see them, who always delighted to roam
Over the Hill where so often together we trod,
When the winds of wild autumn strewed summer's dead leaves
    on the sod,
Ere your steps turned home?

Vera as an undergraduate in May 1915, shortly before she went down to train as a VAD. Vera is in the second row from the back, fifth from the left. The novelist Dorothy L. Sayers is first left in the same row. Four years later Vera returned to a very different university

THE LAMENT OF THE DEMOBILISED

'Four years,' some say consolingly,
   'Oh well,
What's that? You're young. And then it must have been
A very fine experience for you!'
And they forget
How others stayed behind and just got on—
Got on the better since we were away.
And we came home and found
They had achieved, and men revered their names,
But never mentioned ours;
And no one talked heroics now, and we
Must just go back and start again once more.
'You threw four years into the melting-pot—
Did you indeed!' these others cry.
   'Oh well,
The more fool you!'
And we're beginning to agree with them.

ANNIVERSARIES

They come again, strange ghosts of days long dead,
Wreathed with the shadowy joys that once we knew
When withered hair was gold, and pale lips red.

Strange ghosts of days long dead, that we lived through
When Love was young, with shining rose-crowned head,
Ere 'mid our flowers the bitter grief-herb grew.

From regions whither all our dreams are fled,
That aching wounds, long hid, may bleed anew,
They come again, strange ghosts of days long dead.

Vera, *circa* 1925

THE SUPERFLUOUS WOMAN

Ghosts crying down the vistas of the years,
Recalling words
Whose echoes long have died;
And kind moss grown
Over the sharp and blood-bespattered stones
Which cut our feet upon the ancient ways.

But who will look for my coming?

Long busy days where many meet and part;
Crowded aside
Remembered hours of hope;
And city streets
Grown dark and hot with eager multitudes
Hurrying homeward whither respite waits.

But who will seek me at nightfall?

Light fading where the chimneys cut the sky;
Footsteps that pass,
Nor tarry at my door.
And far away,
Behind the row of crosses, shadows black
Stretch out long arms before the smouldering sun.

But who will give me my children?

THE UNSEEN UNDERGRADUATES

(ARMISTICE DAY, 1920)

They'll steal across the darkened quads to-night,
And clasp each other by the hand, and use
The old endearing names, and talk of days
Before the stormy time, when battle's blaze
Called them to leave the haunts of golden years,
And idly dreaming Muse.

They'll flit unseen amid the shadows grey
Beneath some ivied window once their own,
Whereof they dreamed on summer days in France,
With wistful eyes before the great advance,
Knowing in death that other hands would reap
The harvest they had sown.

Their day has passed, but they shall never pass;
They stand behind our urgent stream of life
Half-smiling and half-sad; the chapel hymn
Thrills with a deeper undertone, the dim
Half-realised whisper of their War-won peace
Beyond our lesser strife.

WE SHALL COME NO MORE

So then we came to the Island,
Lissom and young, with the radiant sun in our faces;
Anchored in long quiet lines the ships were waiting,
Giants asleep in the peace of the dark-blue harbour.
Ashore we leapt, to seek the magic adventure
Up the valley at noontide,
Where shimmering lay the fields of asphodel.

O Captain of our Voyage,
What of the Dead?
Dead days, dead hopes, dead loves, dead dreams, dead sorrows—
O Captain of our Voyage,
Do the Dead walk again?

To-day we look for the Island,
Older, a little tired, our confidence waning;
On the ocean bed the shattered ships lie crumbling
Where lost men's bones gleam white in the shrouded silence.
The Island waits, but we shall never find it,
Nor see the dark-blue harbour
Where twilight falls on fields of asphodel.

St George's Hospital and Bay, Malta

THE WAR GENERATION: AVE

In cities and in hamlets we were born,
    And little towns behind the van of time;
A closing era mocked our guileless dawn
    With jingles of a military rhyme.
But in that song we heard no warning chime,
    Nor visualised in hours benign and sweet
The threatening woe that our adventurous feet
    Would starkly meet.

Thus we began, amid the echoes blown
    Across our childhood from an earlier war,
Too dim, too soon forgotten, to dethrone
    Those dreams of happiness we thought secure;
While, imminent and fierce outside the door,
    Watching a generation grow to flower,
The fate that held our youth within its power
    Waited its hour.

Edward

Victor

Roland

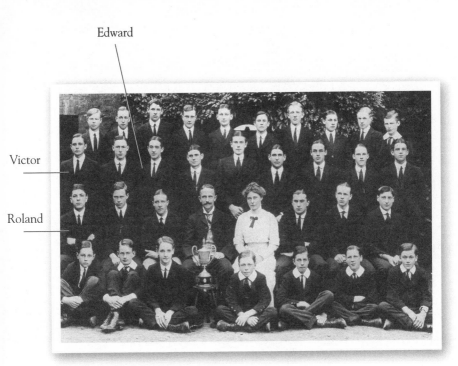

The Lodge, Uppingham School, summer 1914

Roland Leighton's gravestone at Louvencourt photographed by
Vera Brittain in 1921

THE WAR GENERATION: VALE

We, whom the storm-winds battered, come again
Like strangers to the places we have known,
Who sought men's understanding all in vain
For hardened hearts to grief's dark image grown;
So, passing through the careless crowd alone,
Ghosts of a time no future can restore,
We desolately roam for evermore
An empty shore.

For us they live till life itself shall end,
The frailties and the follies of those years,
Their strength which only pride of loss could lend,
Their vanished hopes, their sorrows and their tears;
But slowly towards the verge the dim sky clears,
For nobler men may yet redeem our clay
When we and war together, one wise day,
Have passed away.

PART TWO

PROSE

Vera begins her VAD nursing at the
Devonshire Hospital in Buxton, 1915

The encampment at Etaples

24TH GENERAL HOSPITAL,
BRITISH EXPEDITIONARY FORCE,
FRANCE

17 AUGUST 1917

Having served as a VAD in Buxton, London and Malta, Vera accepted a further foreign posting in the summer of 1917, this time to Etaples in northern France. The following piece, written for St. Monica's School Notes, her old school magazine (which had also printed several of her poems), as one of a number of contributions by old girls who were engaged in war work, expresses the excitement of being close to the Western Front for the first time. The article also marks an important staging post on Vera's journey towards internationalism, and her eventual conversion to Christian pacifism twenty years later. The German prisoners she was nursing, she realised with growing conviction, should not be regarded as the enemy, but rather as suffering humanity.

———

I had rather a bad crossing on the 3rd – somewhat mitigated by the fact that a Major-General of the Staff gave up his cabin to six of us, and I was one of the lucky ones and spent the night at an hotel in Boulogne as there was no train to take us here until the next afternoon.

On the morning of the 4th I went to a most beautiful service at the English Church in Boulogne, in memory of our dead of these three years' war.

The preacher was the Chaplain-in-Chief, who had just come from the Flanders front, and the congregation was entirely officers and men and nurses.

That afternoon I, and four others who had crossed with me, had a train journey of about an hour and then a long muddy walk through a filthy but picturesque little French town in order to arrive at this hospital. The hospital is an enormous place, all huts and canvas; it extends on both sides of a wide main road, nearly at the top of a hill, and almost surrounded by thin woods. The whole place – there are other hospitals and camps here – is known as the 'advanced clearing station', which means that when in a push the casualty clearing stations overflow, we act as one. This is supposed to be one of the best camp hospitals there are. You can imagine how busy we have been during the last push. I work in a hut and sleep under canvas – not in a tent though, but in a little shanty made of canvas and wood.

Of course I am using all my camp equipment, as the little erection which I share with another VAD was quite empty except for a few nails. I am becoming accustomed to and quite amused at the way a candle lantern drops grease on your head when you are least expecting it, or a canvas basin runs out at one end when you pick it up by the other to empty it, or the caterpillars and earwigs find the vicinity of my bed a pleasant refuge when the rain comes on. My companion, however, does not take readily to camp life and gets very fussed. I often long for Stella to share this quite delightful and entertaining life with me, though so far I have been much too busy to be lonely.

I am very lucky in this hospital as the Matron is quite the most charming of the many matrons I have had dealings with, being tall and pretty and very young looking, in spite of a South African ribbon, with a sweet smile and a delightful manner. The Sister in my ward, too, is one of the nicest I have ever worked under.

You may be surprised to hear that I am nursing German prisoners for the present. This hospital is very cosmopolitan as it takes both surgical and medical cases of British and Colonial officers and men, German prisoner officers and men, and Portuguese officers.

My ward is known as the 'German . . . surgical ward'. Every worse case comes to us; we have 33 beds, 7 officers and 26 men. The ward is full of head, chest and abdominal wounds, amputations, and compound complications of the femur, so you can imagine what the work is like. A good many have penetrating wounds, *i.e.*, some internal organ pierced and infected, and these are always very dangerous and difficult cases.

There is a theatre attached to the ward, where we have anything up to 18 operations a day, either from our own ward or from the marquees where the other wounded prisoners are. We take all the worst operation cases.

The staff of the ward, including all the theatre work, is a Sister and myself, one English orderly, and two or three German prisoners who act as orderlies, and certainly work excellently.

Malta changed my ideas of the amount of work and responsibility an individual can be capable of, but this changes it still more. While the theatre is going on I have a great many of the dressings to do; tremendous things, we should have got very excited over in London in the old days; the Sister said to-day: 'You would not find worse cases anywhere than ours.' Bad as the wounds at the 1st London General were after the Somme push, they were nothing to the dreadful wounds these prisoners have – yet here you have one VAD coping with a heavy ward, while in England about six are tumbling over one another in a light one. I am very thankful to be one of the former variety. Had I known I was to have nursed Germans I might have disliked the idea, but I find nothing to dislike in the fact, for I have never been so genuinely interested in hospital work before.

Of course I love living at top speed, and a push elates me.

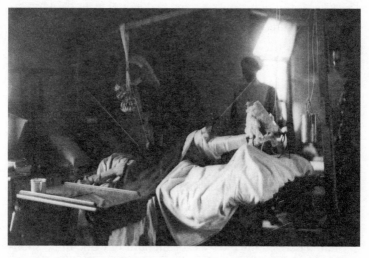

Nurses at the bedside of a patient at the 24 General, Etaples

These Germans, with one or two flagrant exceptions, are quite decent people, and very grateful for anything you do for them. It is a strange and interesting experience to be nursing the enemy, and gives one an opportunity of living up to our motto, which I have always liked so much, 'Inter Arma Caritas'. Anyhow, even if one wanted to hate the poor things, it would be quite impossible as they are far too ill; one forgets that they are the enemy, and can only remember that they are suffering human beings.

I have never seen so many deaths as I have in these last ten days.

My half-forgotten, but reviving German, is extremely useful as the Sister does not speak it, while very few of the officers and none of the men speak English.

From a surgical point of view the work is quite enthralling, it is by far the most advanced I have ever seen or done.

We have a charming MO, who is always teaching me things by the way; also attached to the ward as anaesthetist and assistant MO is a German prisoner officer, who before the war was an almost fully qualified medical student, quite a nice person, a Saxon who hates the Prussians, and from him I learn quite a lot of both German and surgery, also some very interesting things about Germany and German people, which, of course, I cannot repeat here. Whenever I go on duty I have not either the slightest feeling of reluctance or boredom, which has never happened before in hospital work.

Even from a political point of view I cannot get up any animosity towards my patients, it is hard to reconcile, especially among the men, what one knows of them with what one has heard about German warfare. One can only feel that, like all of us in this present unhappy world, they are the poor victims of that intolerable caste and system we are fighting to destroy.

But when I think of Edward in one part of France working to annihilate these very same people that I in another part am working to save, I begin to realise the folly and tragedy of war in a way I never did before.

There is a great coming and going along our road all day long, transports, ambulances and troops travelling from one place 'Somewhere in France' to another. We hear all sorts of martial music – sometimes the skirling of bagpipes as a Highland regiment marches past.

There is a great glamour about this road at night, with the glow of lighted huts and tents on either side, and the transport lights coming out of the distance and disappearing into it again. Further up the road at the end of a wood below some sand hills is a big military cemetery, forest of wooden crosses stretching right down to the sea. Each long low mound is covered with a mass of gay-coloured flowers, marigolds, nasturtiums or Iceland poppies; it is one of the loveliest places I have ever been in.

THE ASIAGO PLATEAU

After leaving Oxford, in the summer of 1921, Vera and her friend Winifred Holtby, who she had met on returning to Somerville in 1919, took a six-week holiday in Italy and France. The primary purpose of their trip was to visit the graves of Vera's fiancé Roland Leighton at Louvencourt on the Somme, and of her brother Edward, buried in the remote military cemetery at Granezza, in northern Italy, four thousand feet up on the Asiago Plateau, where he had been killed in June 1918. On the morning of 7 September 1921, Vera and Winifred began their perilous ascent of the Plateau.

———

Until the King and Queen made their pilgrimage to the British graves in Italy the English public knew little of the Asiago Plateau but the Royal Visit has recalled to many minds the name of Europe's highest battlefield.

A few hours' journey from Venice, between the rich valleys of the Brenta and the Piave, the heights of Asiago rise like a grey cloud into the sky. Their summits, pine-clad and remote, witnessed the final struggle of Italians and Austrians in the last year of the Great War. Beside the Italians fought a few British and French Divisions, which were sent to stiffen the Italian defence after the Caporetto disaster in October 1917. The grandeur of the Plateau is too inaccessible to be familiar. Even the inhabitants of

Bassano, which lies at the foot of Asiago, know little of the battle-fields, though they shuddered for months beneath the roar of the Austrian guns.

In the main street of Bassano stands a small white hotel, the haunt of an Italian touring club. The proprietor speaks no English but he is charmingly voluble in broken French. He explains that he has a motor car to lend of a power that will even climb the rough road to Asiago. The bargain is soon completed and the open car sets out.

Villages that grow thinner as the ascent grows steeper, cluster at intervals round the first few miles of the road. Then the sheer mountain-side towers above the car, and the hair-pin bends of the unwalled road become more terrifying as the Brenta Valley far away fades into a blue-green mist pierced with a streak of silver.

At last, after a climb that seems to have lasted for hours the road grows more level. Vineyards and villages have long disap-peared; the narrow track is winding now between the grey rocks and pine forests that stretch into infinity. The air is cold; there are no flowers, no heather. The whole world is green and grey, and marvellously still. Then the suave voice of the chauffeur offers the surprising information that the car has reached the scene of the Austrian advance of 1917.

A sudden recollection of the devastated areas of France flashes inevitably into the mind. Is not this lonely plateau the devastated area of Italy? But where are the fields ploughed by shells into a grim travesty of Nature, where the broken spectre-like trees and the sordid heaps of rust-red barbed-wire and bully beef tins?

The Asiago Plateau is not a devastated area; it never has been and never could have been. Shells once split the grey rocks, but only to add a few scars to those already made by time and climate, a few sharp stones to the roughness of the road. Shells once tore screaming through the pine woods, as the long thin trunks piled in hundreds by the wayside bear witness. But no gaps are conspicuous in the thickness of the forest; the pines can still be counted by none but the All-Knowing, who alone can number the hairs of a man's head. Now and again a rough tangle of barbed wire climbs like an alien plant over the rocks, with the ruins of a dug-out crouching half-hidden beneath. Sometimes a mountain tarn disguises the rude disfigurement of a shell-hole; sometimes the trail of Austrian trenches still winds serpent-like along a distant hill. But these incongruous traces of strife seem only to emphasize the silent scorn of the Plateau for war's feverish folly; they do not detract from that grim imperturbable majesty which guns could not annihilate nor the tramp of armies deface.

At the highest corner of the Plateau where the pine-woods are thickest, the car comes to a standstill. Here in the depth of the forest, the earth hides the bones of those British soldiers who fell on this loftiest of foreign fields. These military cemeteries are small, and of a snowy whiteness against their background of sombre green. Sometimes their stone walls enclose as few as fifty graves; none of them contain so many as two-hundred. At the head of each cemetery stands a cenotaph surmounted by a cross, bearing the now familiar inscription 'Their name liveth for evermore'. The names upon the stones belong for the most part to the men who fell in the great battle waged among the pine-woods on June 15th 1918.

The rocks and the pines have lent their austere dignity to these little graveyards. In summer and autumn, small hardy ferns cluster round the foot of each white stone, but the gay flowers which deck the military cemeteries of France cannot live on so high an altitude. Only when winter is past, the brave spring Alpines burst through the iron earth, blossoming in their wild beauty upon the resting places of those who knew only the springtime of the year.

At last the low sun, slanting through sullen clouds, heralds the hour of departure. It is strangely difficult to bid farewell to the graves of the British soldiers, strangely difficult to overcome the fantastic longing to keep them company in their loneliness. As the car turns the corner to plunge steeply downhill into the volatile life of the valley, one last backward glance yearns towards the grave dark pines, jealously hiding in their heart their alien treasure, the white memorials of youth immortalised by death.

OUR BACKS TO THE WALL

A MEMORY OF THE WAR

By 1928, when she published this article in the Manchester Guardian, *Vera was both a successful journalist and writer with two novels to her name, and an ardent campaigner for feminism and the League of Nations Union. She was married, to the political scientist G.E.G. Catlin, and had recently given birth to a son, John Edward. Vera shared her London home with Winifred Holtby. Winifred was also politically active in the women's and peace movements, as well as in South African affairs, and was the author of three novels which contributed to her growing reputation as a writer.*

'Our Backs to the Wall' was prompted by the death, at the end of January 1928, of Earl Haig who, as Douglas Haig, had been Commander-in-Chief of the British Army on the Western Front in 1916–18.

———

Nearly ten years ago, on the evening of 21 March 1918, an Army Sister and I – then a very youthful and ardent VAD – were walking among the yellow sandhills on the French coast close to Etaples. Both of us worked on the staff of a large base hospital, celebrated in those days throughout the British Army, but of which all trace is now covered by the gorse and scrub that has grown over the old camps along the main railway line from Boulogne to Paris. The

Sister is now the superintendent of a military hospital in India, while my own endeavours to combine marriage with the career of a writer have removed me very far from the nursing world in which I spent four strenuous years of unintended experience. Those years have vanished into the past and nothing is left of them – nothing except the crowded cemetery at Etaples and a host of memories.

Vera in the 1920s

Memories, however, last longer than war, and often longer than man. I can still recall vividly the queer menace of that evening among the sandhills; everything was wrapped in an unearthly stillness, and even the waves breaking upon the shore appeared to make no sound. A copper glow surrounded the setting sun, which hung like an angry ball of fire in the midst of a battalion of thunderous clouds; it reminded us, I remember, of the superstitions that were rife in the first days of the war, when people said that they had seen blood upon the sun and moon. We returned to the camp to learn that the rumours of the morning were confirmed, and that the great German offensive had begun.

The days that followed are a confused recollection of convoys, ambulances, operations, evacuations to England, and the continuous sounding of the 'fall-in'. The hut of which I then had sole charge had been hitherto used for light medical cases; it was hastily converted into a surgical ward during the night, and I came on duty the next morning to find all the beds occupied, and the floor covered with stretchers, scattered boots, muddy khaki and other hastily removed remnants of field service kit. Ten cases were marked down for immediate operation and a dozen more for x-ray. I remember gazing ruefully at the solitary pair of forceps standing in their jar of methylated spirit which constituted the entire range of my surgical equipment. Fortunately for myself I burst out laughing, and ran to bombard a half-frantic dispensary with the gay feeling that one gets when catastrophe has advanced beyond the utmost limit of human capacity to cope with it.

Day after day some fresh conquest of our adversaries was whispered first with bated breath and then published tentatively abroad. Péronne, Bapaume, Beaumont Hamel and finally Albert itself, fell into German hands; even Armentières, British for so long, had to be evacuated owing to the gas from exploding shells. From the fog of unreliable rumour which always covers the progress of a great retreat came the fear of a permanent break-through, and at Etaples preparations were made for the flight that before long might become necessary for us all. As the battle surged closer, the boom of the guns, a sense rather than a sound, shook the earth by day and night, and when darkness had fallen flashes of light could be seen on the horizon. From nearer at hand the air was filled with a dense and deafening roar; trains with reinforcements thundered all day up the line or lumbered down more slowly with their heavy freight of wounded; motor lorries and ammunition waggons crashed endlessly up the road. Occasionally the wounded – who escaped in anything that would pick them up, from staff cars to cattle trucks – were accompanied by Sisters fleeing from the captured casualty clearing stations; more often they arrived with no attendants at all and with the first field-dressing still unchanged. Only too frequently it was dead men whom the orderlies lifted out of the trains, and many a time the more serious cases had to be cut off the stretchers on which they had lain with their inadequately covered wounds undressed for many hours.

Three weeks of such sights and sounds, of fourteen-hour days without off-duty time and with frequent calls at night, will blunt the edge of the youngest and most adventurous spirit. Weariness of limbs and sickness of soul had engendered the despairing sense that nothing mattered except to end the strain one way or another; victory and defeat seemed to be, after all, very much the same thing. As it happened, this impression was correct; but fortunately for their duties in the last months of the war, it was not until two or three years afterwards that the men and women who took part in it were to learn for good that lesson of disillusion.

On 10 April a few fellow-workers and I stumbled through the long camp to the Sisters' quarters for our midday meal with the certainty that we could not go on – and saw, pinned up on the notice-board, Lord Haig's famous 'order of the day'. Standing there, with our weariness and our hunger strangely diminished, we read the words which put heart into so many whose need of endurance was far greater than ours:

> There is no course open to us but to fight it out. Every position must be held to the last man; there must be no retirement. With our backs to the wall and believing in the justice of our cause, each one of us must fight to the end. The safety of our homes and the freedom of mankind depend alike upon the conduct of each one of us at this critical moment.

Most of those who were reading, at any rate among the VADs, belonged to that generation which has grown into womanhood with a scorn of showing its feelings and a reluctance to admit even their existence; but fatigue had made us vulnerable to emotion, and we left the notice-board fired with a tearful and glowing determination. Whatever our private views about war, we were then in the midst of it, and individuals – whether fighters or merely workers – who are faced with the alternatives of resistance and collapse seldom stop to argue the merits of the case until afterwards. No doubt we were all mad, and a noble madness is the most dangerous form of insanity; the fact remains that it was nobility at which we aimed, and nobility that Lord Haig's order enabled us for the time to achieve.

A month later the crisis was over, and I went home on leave. For the best part of six weeks, off-duty hours and walks to Le Touquet had been unattainable; my eyes had seen nothing but the long huts and the stretcher cases on the beds and along the trampled floor. Looking out of the train window as we passed through the woods and glades that surround Hardelot, the green veil flung over the trees and the yellow gleam of daffodils in the grass startled me into amazement, and I almost wept with joy as I realized that, like a thief in the night, the spring had come.

THEIR NAME LIVETH

FORGETTING WOMEN'S WAR-WORK

In November 1929, after many false starts, Vera finally began to write the book about her war experiences that would be published, in 1933, as Testament of Youth. *This article, one of several that she was to write for the* Manchester Guardian *in the next few years to commemorate Armistice Day, anticipated a major theme of her famous autobiography, namely, that women's contribution to the war effort deserved to be properly represented in its literature.*

––––––––

Through our cities and towns and villages on Armistice Day, we meet to revive our memories – now slipping further back into an ever dimmer past – of ten, eleven, twelve years ago. In London we file past the grave of the Unknown Warrior and lay wreaths on the Cenotaph. In the larger towns which possess cathedrals or important churches, some part of these has usually been transformed with the War Memorial, and here we gather quietly for the silence, bowing our heads and dipping our flags. But in the smaller towns and villages a hill-side or a village green, along which everybody passes, has often been thought more appropriate than the tiny church for the site of the memorial cross or cenotaph which records the sacrifice that was none the less bitter

An draft plan for an early version of *Testament of Youth*, entitled 'This Was Their War'. It was to have been a novel, based on Vera's experiences, and would have included several of Roland's poems for having been demanded from a mere handful of obscure individuals.

Perhaps because the soldiers whom they commemorate were for the most part simple men, who died in a simple faith that knew nothing of the economic intrigues and the secret treaties which are the motive power of modern warfare, these village crosses have become hallowed oases endowed with a strangely moving serenity that touches the heart more deeply than the elaborate memorials in the churches. The memories that they inspire, completely dissociated from sect or dogma, somehow seem more personal and poignant.

I passed by one of them only the other day, as I walked over a wooded hill near Pangbourne on a Sunday morning. Devoted hands had just arranged two tall green vases of red and golden autumn flowers on either side of the cross, but a strong breeze was blowing, and one of the vases had fallen over, casting the bright dahlias and daisies untidily down the steps of the little platform. When I had refilled the vase and gathered up and replaced the flowers – an action which seemed more truly a sacrament than any that the church bells ringing in the valley would have demanded of me – I read the brief tale of names on the cross. And as I had expected, and as is the case in ninety-nine out of every hundred of these memorials, the names inscribed were all names of men.

'Where war,' wrote Olive Schreiner in *Woman and Labour*, 'has been to preserve life, or land, or freedom, unparasitized and labouring women have in all ages known how to bear an active part, and die.' In the Great War, which they then believed to be waged for freedom, the women of this country knew how to bear an active part; they accepted gladly the strain and the burden and the small rewards, though many of them were throwing off parasitism for the first time. But for the most part they did not die. The war was not fought on their soil, and when they served abroad, the tradition that sets, even in wartime, the exaggerated values of sentiment upon individual female life, protected the majority of them in their own despite against the ravages of aerial bomb and submarine torpedo. They worked, but they also went on living and suffering and remembering; and immortality – as so many of the disabled and the unemployed have since had reason to realize – is the reward only of a life laid down. In wartime it is necessary to die in order that one's name shall live for evermore.

For this reason the large number of war-records that have taken shape during the past eleven years in literature, in painting and in sculpture have in general ignored the active war-work done by the women. There are, of course, exceptions, such as the curiously repellent statue of Nurse Cavell above Trafalgar Square, and the vivid description in *The Well of Loneliness* of women ambulance drivers at the front. I am told that the lovely Edinburgh War Memorial has a window dedicated to the women doctors and nurses and auxiliary corps and land-workers, while records of these activities exist along with the rest in the cloistered peace of the Imperial War Museum. But for the most part war memorials, war paintings and war literature reveal to a later generation only the work and agony of the men, because this was crowned and immortalized by death.

The absence of allusion to women's work in the better-known examples of war literature may perhaps be attributed to the fact that the best-known plays and novels have so far been contributed by men. It is men who therefore predominate in the batch of contemporaneous German war novels which have recently acquired such fame, and men who hold the stage exclusively in the play *Journey's End*, which owes so much of its worldwide triumph to its unpretentious photography. In so far as women have been included in war literature at all, they have appeared chiefly in the role of passive sufferer – that role which is so poignantly expressed in the beautiful and too little known lines of May Wedderburn Cannan:

When the Vision dies in the dust of the market-place,
When the light is dim,
When you lift up your eyes and cannot behold his face,
When your heart is far from him,
Know this is your War; in this loneliest hour you ride
Down the Roads he knew;
Though he comes no more at night, he will kneel at your
    side
For comfort to dwell with you.

One or two of the best-known English war novels have failed to recognize even thus far the wartime heritage of pain which comes through their wifehood or motherhood to the great majority of women. In *Death of a Hero*, for instance, Mr Richard Aldington savagely attacked both these relationships, exploding in a cynical fury of scorn what seemed to him the myth of their sanctity. His two 'heroines', Elizabeth and Fanny, like the mother of his 'hero', George Winterbourne, create the illusion that the normal part played by woman in wartime was that of a luxurious parasite battening upon the sufferings of much-enduring man. The same impression is left by Major Acland's story of the Canadian troops, *All Else is Folly*, which actually takes for its text the words of the misogynist Nietzsche in *Thus Spake Zarathustra*: 'Man shall be trained for war and women for the recreation of the warrior; all else is folly.'

Details of women's activity in wartime exist of course in government blue-books, such as the reports of the Women's Employment Committee and of the War Cabinet Committee on Women in Industry, but records in this form are virtually buried in so far as the man and woman in the street are concerned. They exercise no popular influence, and strike no chord of recollection; they arouse respect and admiration in no one but the patient research-worker. Even the argument that the various Acts which have enfranchised and opened the professions to women are the real memorial to their war-time achievements does not really hold good, for these Acts were the logical consequences of the feminist movement, and though the war hastened them they would in any case have come in time.

The active part played by women in the Great War requires its own poet or novelist or dramatist, who will transform the dry sentences of government reports into living words before the memories of 1914 to 1918 pass into oblivion with the war generation.

THE REAL VAD

FROM FANCY BACK TO FACT

The writer May Wedderburn Cannan, whose wartime service included a stint as a VAD in an Oxford hospital, later recalled the 'mocking opposition' that VADs had faced when the programme was established. 'The uniform was ugly and what did we think we could do?' As the war continued, though, the image of the VAD as a heroic exemplar quickly took hold, overcoming initial scepticism about the motives and usefulness of the women who volunteered. A clipping from the Spectator, *preserved by Vera between the pages of her diary in December 1915, praised the 'thousands of girls' who had led 'easy and cloistered lives' before the war, for not quailing before the experience of being 'pitchforked . . . into hospitals full of men maimed and disfigured by terrible and repulsive wounds'.*

However, by the early thirties, as the following article shows, something of that negative stereotyping had reasserted itself in the lurid descriptions of a VAD's life contained in war books like Brigadier-General Crozier's memoir, A Brass Hat in No Man's Land *(1930). In this piece Vera emphasizes the essential respectability of the VAD in terms not dissimilar to those employed during the war by Dame Katharine Furse, Commander-in-Chief of the Voluntary Aid Detachment, who was intent on defending her nurses against any accusations of 'unladylike' behaviour.*

————

The present tendency of some women's war books is certainly to be regretted. For a long time women refrained from contributing any record of their adventures at all, and up to a few months ago, Mary Borden's *The Forbidden Zone* and Mary Lee's *It's A Great War!* remained the only description of individual feminine experience which had acquired either sales or reputation. These two are still the only war by women worthy to be considered in the same category as Edmund Blunden's *Undertones of War*, Richard Aldington's

Vera in Buxton before the war

Death of a Hero and other serious works on the war by men, but the impression that they made has lately been eclipsed by that of such fast-selling and far more lurid stories as *WAAC* and *Not So Quiet*.

The earlier war books by men had created an appetite – fortunately now diminishing – for first-hand horrors which women who mostly remained miles from the trenches could not hope to supply, so it was perhaps inevitable that one or two women authors, anxious to pander to the popular taste for sensation, should endeavour to create the impression that even though women could not appear in the front line they did not lack devastating experiences of quite another kind. I am now told, though I have not read it, that a book by a man – Brigadier-General Crozier's *A Brass Hat In No Man's Land* – contributes its quota to the growing legend of sex-debauched females who donned the uniform of VAD, WAAC or ambulance driver merely as a prelude to emotional excesses of the wildest description.

Probably because I happened to be one of those VADs who served for the greater part of the war without witnessing one single episode that could possibly be described as an orgy, I find these fiery fables of sex-mad hospital workers peculiarly exasperating. Their acceptance is no doubt assisted by the fact that the recollection of what actually constituted a VAD has now become somewhat shadowy, and is further confused by the different kinds of voluntary war-nurse that existed at the time. These ranged from the unofficial and irregular habituée of small local hospitals, who donned a uniform chiefly because she thought it becoming, who confined her activities to arranging flowers and smoothing pillows, and who had not the slightest intention of tying herself to duties that were either permanent or unpleasant, to the full-fledged member of a Voluntary Aid Detachment, complete with First Aid and Home Nursing certificates and the experience of preliminary weeks of training in a civilian hospital, who passed (for the magnificent salary of £20 a year plus £2 for uniform) entirely under the control of the Army Nursing Service, renewed her contract every six months, and was liable in the same way as an RANC orderly to military orders involving either home or foreign service.

The latter kind of volunteer nurse had – not without occasional justification – considerable contempt for the former, and it is unfortunate that the same popular term should have come to be applied to both. If, indeed, 'orgies' of the kind indicated ever actually took place, I suspect that they happened at luxurious little hospitals where there were too many nurses and not enough occupation, rather than at the usually understaffed Stationary and General Army Hospitals, where for a considerable part of every year off-duty time was the exception rather than the rule.

As one of the full-time VADs attached to the Army Nursing Service both at home and abroad, I had, I think, a fairly representative experience. My weeks of preliminary nursing were done at the Devonshire Hospital in Buxton from June to October 1915; my orders then took me, for nearly a year in each place, to the 1st London General Hospital in Camberwell, St George's Hospital in Malta, and the 24th General Hospital at Etaples. After that family circumstances demanded a long leave, and I finished my war service, in April 1919, with short periods at two London hospitals, St Thomas's and Millbank.

At none of these five great military hospitals did I come across one example of a VAD being sent home on account of a prospective illegitimate baby, or even, so far as I remember, for any form of sexual indiscretion. That indiscretions did sometimes occur it is of course impossible to doubt; now and again we were solemnly catechised by

Recruitment poster for VADs

an embarrassed Matron with regard to disreputable incidents – of which the disreputableness was greatly exaggerated by the importance attached to it – that were alleged to have happened in our particular area. Such incidents and such conduct were, however, rare and inconspicuous; they played no such part in the life of the average hospital as some of the war writers would have us believe.

The majority of VADs were, like myself, very young and quite unsophisticated. When we first joined up our chief preoccupation was the fear of being turned down for incompetence after the month-on-trial with which every voluntary nurse's Army career began. Disturbed far more by the unfamiliarity of our duties than by sex complications, we were childishly and ardently conscientious; inspired by a pathetically high patriotic idealism, we had a touching faith in the righteousness of our cause and the disinterested Olympian virtue of such wartime leaders as French Jellicoe, Foch and Mr Lloyd George. This type of mentality may be consistent with nervous over-exertion and unnecessary self-sacrifice, but it is quite incompatible with emotional orgies and physical excess.

If, however, in some distant future another international war should come to pass despite the efforts of those of us who are working to avert it, there are two characteristics of Army nursing service that I should like to see completely altered. One is the absurd segregation of the men and women working in hospital units. I sometimes begin to doubt the accuracy of my own recollections when I remember that during our fortnight's voyage to Malta via Mudros on the hospital ship *Britannic* (doomed to be torpedoed on its very next voyage) the Sisters and VADs were portentously separated from the medical officers and orderlies by a rope stretched across the deck; or when I recall the mingled agonies of apprehension and conscience that accompanied the surreptitious but otherwise entirely wholesome and invigorating afternoons spent in playing tennis at the medical officers' quarters during a period of night duty in Malta. Such emotional catastrophes as did occur were due, I am convinced, mainly to the tempting and tormenting suggestiveness of this unnatural segregation.

In the second place I hope that the women workers in any future war will be spared the agonising conflict between national and family claims which caused them far greater distress than any of the strange and strenuous tasks that fell upon them. Called home from France against my will by a domestic crisis just after the great retreat of 1918, I can never forget the conscience-stricken resentment aroused in me by the challenging posters in Trafalgar Square, proclaiming that my country needed women for the WAAC, the WRNS and the WRAF. Sons achieve, in both war and peace, a merciful immunity from demands of maternal breakdowns or the after-effects of paternal influenza, but as long as convention declares that daughters, whether engaged in peacetime professions or wartime service, must always be accessible, so long will parents allow themselves to become panicky and dependent. To most women in wartime, conscription would seem merciful. The demands of most war-work are sufficient to exercise all their powers, without the additional strain of those incompatible claims which were responsible far more often than indiscreet love affairs for physical collapse or emotional distress.

A POPPY FOR HER COT

SOME ARMISTICE REFLECTIONS

Another of Vera's Armistice Day pieces, published in the Manchester
Guardian *in 1930. This one depicts Vera's two young children, three-
year-old John Edward, and Shirley, born just three months earlier, and
asks how the war generation can warn the coming generation about the false
glamour of war.*

———————

The other day I overheard a curiously significant conversation
between my nurse and my two children. Nurse, a buxom, bright-
faced young woman of twenty, was correcting an adjustable
calendar, transposed by the roving fingers of John Edward, who
now, by standing on the fender, can just reach the mantelpiece.

'Why, John!' I heard her cheerfully remark. 'It's the first of
November! Soon it'll be November the eleventh. Then we'll get
John a big, big poppy – and Shirley can have a poppy for her cot!'

'A poppy for her cot!' My mind echoed stupidly the words that
had struck so sharply upon my affronted ears. Did this young
woman, my outraged memories demanded, so utterly lack imag-
ination that she really proposed to attach that symbol of grim
death to the frill of yellow muslin which shielded my baby daugh-
ter's innocent head from the colder winds of Heaven?

John Edward and Shirley

And then, more reasonably, I remembered that the twelve years which have carried the war generation from its earliest youth into its thirties have bridged for its successors the far wider gulf between childhood and adulthood. My nurse was only eight when the first Armistice Day fell with such a strange silence upon the deafening clamour of a world at arms; she was only four when the tread of hostile armies marching across Europe to destroy one another first sounded in the thrilled ears of our younger selves, boys and girls just home from our years at school.

Why, then, should I so resent the fact that she sees in the sale of Flanders poppies merely a rather superior Flag Day? For her the Armistice belongs to those periodic national celebrations which began before her awareness of the world had developed into a conscious realization of its meaning. It has taken its place, with Trafalgar and Waterloo, in the sequence of historical events for which she and her contemporaries were in no way responsible; like Mafeking and Ladysmith for us, it is associated in her mind with ancient songs and long-ago conversations emerging from the dim shadows of early childhood.

And to my children, I reflected, it will not even be this. On my mantelpiece beside the calendar which Nurse so cheerfully adjusted, stands the photograph of a second lieutenant in uniform – a portrait of the children's uncle, my young brother, who has lain these dozen years in his grave on the Asiago Plateau, but who – apart from the fact that every year he seems to grow more curiously juvenile to be my brother – is as real to me as he was in 1914. I realize with a shock that he was killed in action nine years before John Edward was born, and that to my boy and girl he will be but a name, a legend, scarcely distinguishable in their dawning imaginations from Kingsley's fabulous heroes, the sons of the Immortals, who went forth to fight the Titans and monsters, the enemies of gods and men. Each year a poppy is sadly placed in a vase before his photograph; this year a poppy will jubilantly decorate my little daughter's cot. It is all one to Nurse and the children.

This tale, however, has a moral, for it shows very clearly that memorial celebrations are not enough. Time has a deceptive habit of blurring our pain while preserving the glamour of our larger-scale tragedies. Our tears and our anguish fade into oblivion, but the thrill of catastrophic events, the odd brightness of happy moments shining through the storm-clouds of disaster, keep the same peculiar vividness that they wore in the yesterday to which they belong. And Nature herself conspires with time to cheat our recollections; grass has grown over the shell-holes at Ypres, and the cultivated meadows of industrious peasants have replaced the hut-scarred fields at Etaples and Camiers where once I nursed the wounded in the great retreat of 1918.

By what means shall we recall to life our grief and our terror, in order that posterity may recognize them for what they were? It cannot be, at best, an easy task, for nothing is more profoundly true than the fact that an individual usually differs far more from his or her self of fifteen years ago than from any contemporary. We have done so many things since the war, learnt so much in a world of which the artificial conditions of wartime kept us ignorant so much longer than is normal for young men and women. We have worked so hard, some of us almost frantically, to retrieve those lost years, have flung ourselves into causes, founded families, fought for careers, until the war has come to appear to us as an event that happened long ago in the lifetime of somebody else.

Though a mass of literature has already grown up around the war, it is still – despite the fact that the immense civilian armies were more articulate than actual fighters have ever been before – inadequate to save from self-destruction a new generation which is eager, as all new generations are, to despise its elders and disregard their warnings.

The decline of enthusiasm for pacifist movements, the growing strength of aggressive nationalism, the setting up of dictators in one after another of the states of Europe – all these testify to the failure of our ceremonies, our war-books, our peace propaganda as yet to bring about that great reformation which they set out to achieve in the hearts of men. How to preserve the memory of our suffering in such a way that our successors may understand it and refrain from the temptations offered by glamour and glory – this is the problem which we, the war generation, have still to solve before the darkness covers us.

RE-ENCOUNTER

The writing of Testament of Youth *took just over three years. The reconstruction of recent history involved Vera in considerable research. It entailed the careful checking of historical events as well as the unearthing of her own personal records of the war – among them her diary and the letters she had sent to Edward, Roland, Victor and Geoffrey, together with their replies – which she wanted to quote from freely in the book. In 1998 many of these letters were published in full for the first time, under the title* Letters from a Lost Generation.

In September 1932, while she was writing the chapter describing Edward's return to the Front in January 1918, following a bout of leave, Vera had 'a most extraordinary dream', which formed the inspiration for this short story written soon afterwards.

————

She and her mother had been tidying the flat.

'I really must get those books and papers sorted before I take your father to the sea,' Mrs Deane had telephoned. 'There are all Vincent's letters to you and some of David's as well. Can't you let Nurse or Martin take the children for once, and come round this afternoon?'

So Hilary sent Christine out in her pram with Nurse, and left Lancelot playing bricks with his father while she went over to

CAMBERWELL.S.E
12.15 AM
9 NOV 15

CAMBERWELL.S.E
12.15 AM
9 NOV 15

ONE PENNY

Lieut. R. A. Leighton -
7th Worcestershire Regt -
British Expeditionary Force.
France .

94.

Miss V. M. Brittain
V.A.D.
St George's Hospital
Malta
M. E. F.

FIELD
SB

PASSED
CENSOR
806

Kensington. She wouldn't have very long, she reflected, because at six o'clock she was meeting Richard and seeing his boat-train off at the station. But somehow or other the papers got sorted in time, and all the War letters were tied up and put away.

On the whole she was glad that she wouldn't have to see them again; it was so strange to read Vincent's letters from France after being married for seven years to Martin. Did Richard know, she wondered, that David's eager, vivid descriptions of the Front, written to him when the two of them were serving with different battalions of the Sherwood Foresters, had never been thrown away? But she didn't ask her parents, for they hardly mentioned Richard's name nowadays; sometimes they seemed to have forgotten that they had a son at all.

When the papers were finished, she and her mother went down in the lift, and she waited at the door while Mrs Deane brought the car round from the garage. Odd that she didn't know that her mother had bought a car! It was a quaint little model, too, when she came to look at it closely; although it was bright orange, it vaguely resembled a suitcase, and there was certainly something peculiar about the windows. But her mother seemed pleased enough with it as she got in and drove herself away.

Hilary was still speculating about the make of the car, when she met Richard outside the restaurant. It was remarkable, she reflected, how little he had changed all these years, though without having altered in any recognizable fashion he did look older and more depressed. She felt definitely worried about her brother; it was inexplicable that he, of all people, should take an engineering job in India when his sole interest had always been in music. Queer, how completely out of touch with each other they'd become since the War, when they were such perfect companions in the early days. She, of course, was always so busy with her writing, and Martin, and the children, that she felt a little vague as to how exactly Richard *had* put in the time. It was still as a schoolboy, just before the War, that she liked best to remember him, when he'd played the violin so magnificently at the Uppingham concerts, and everyone had said how promising his compositions were. Why hadn't he kept them up? she wondered; he'd always been so keen then, so vital, so resolutely ambitious.

'Whatever did you want to go and do engineering for?' she enquired, as they hailed a taxi and began to drive stationwards through the dreary, colourless streets.

'Why shouldn't I?' commented Richard indifferently, looking with dark, disillusioned eyes at the squalid houses. 'It's as good as anything else.'

It wouldn't have been once, thought Hilary.

'After all,' she volunteered, 'you never really tried to finish Greats, did you – or Music? I always thought it was a pity you didn't go back to Oxford after the War.'

Richard shrugged his shoulders glumly.

'Well,' he remarked, 'they'd hardly have me back there now, would they?'

Wouldn't they? meditated Hilary. Why shouldn't they? After all, he wasn't as old as all that. Twenty-two, was it? . . . Twenty-two . . . Why, good Heavens, how absurd she was! What could she have been thinking about? Richard must be thirty-six now . . . yes, thirty-six. How time raced! After all, she herself was . . . Well, well, best forget about that. It didn't do to worry too much over the passage of time, or else one began to wonder why one hadn't got on quicker one's self, and to lose confidence in the future.

'Do you ever play the violin now?' she inquired, hoping that the old entrancing topic might perhaps soften the morose fixity of his grim, gloomy face. But its lines only deepened.

'No,' he replied shortly. 'It was never much good, you know, after the Somme . . . My arm still hurts at times, and I can't get the finer tones at all.'

'But you do go to concerts just the same?'

No, he assured her, he didn't; not even to them. Somehow he couldn't get up an interest in music now that he wasn't able to play himself any more.

'Oh, Richard!' she exclaimed, bitterly disappointed. 'And I've been to them myself quite a lot because I thought you'd still be enjoying them and we could keep in touch that way!'

'In that case,' he responded, with a stranger's polite, unmoved indifference, 'I must start going again.'

Was there no way at all of getting near him? Hilary wondered desperately. Here was the station in sight; in a few minutes his train would be gone and she might not see him again for years. Turning to him eagerly, she seized his cold, unresponsive hands in her warm fingers.

'Richard, do you really want to go to India? Do you really want this engineering job? It isn't in your line at all, is it?'

But he only disengaged his hands and answered apathetically: 'Oh, it'll do well enough! You have to take what you can get nowadays, you know. Anyhow, what does it matter?' And he stared gloomily at the row of porters as the taxi turned into the station yard.

'Perhaps, after all,' thought Hilary, with a flash of melancholy insight, 'it would have been better for him if he'd been killed in the War, like the others . . .'

There was a sudden thunderous knocking, and she woke with a start to find Margaret, the housemaid, holding out her early morning cup of tea. It took her quite a minute to realize that she was lying beside Martin in her bedroom at home, and that Richard had been killed in action on the mountains above Vicenza, sixteen years ago.

WHILE WE REMEMBER

THE PURPOSE OF ARMISTICE DAY

Vera's final Armistice Day article, published in November 1932, confronts the fear that, after barely more than a decade, this annual day of national commemoration might already be in jeopardy.

———

Once more as Armistice Day comes round – so swiftly, it seems, to those of us who remember as though it were yesterday the startling sound of victorious guns rolling up the river from Westminster – the usual protests against the perpetuation of the ceremony find their way into the press. The Derbyshire vicar who has refused to hold a special service in his parish church is by no means the only exponent of the view that Armistice Day is a dying institution.

This attitude towards the war and its aftermath, like novels of escape, and sweepstakes, and popular interest in society romances, appears to be one more example of the flight from reality which Mr Wyndham Lewis has called 'the supreme immorality of the desire to forget'. It is not a stimulating or a hopeful world which the determined realist faces today, and for those who decide that modern life is too uncomfortable to be honestly faced at all, Armistice Day with its universal poppies and its garlanded war-memorials is full of inconvenient reminders.

Many of us are now drifting into an apathetic indifference which those who cannot remember the war have perhaps never drifted out of – an indifference which ignores the fact that apparently remote political causes have intimate personal effects, and refuses to acknowledge that, in a shrinking world of economically interdependent nations, there is no such thing as complete private irresponsibility for public catastrophe. 'They think Hitler doesn't matter to them so long as there's plenty of dry soap in the house,' a very intelligent north country woman once ruefully remarked to me of her feminine neighbours. If most of us, from the very young to the very old, had not adopted that same attitude twenty years ago, the Great War would probably never have happened, for the peoples would not have permitted their governments to wage it.

On the night of 4 August 1914, I remember standing in the confused darkness of a Buxton street, waiting with a crowd of bewildered men and women for the reply that never came to the British ultimatum to Germany. To me and my contemporaries, with our hitherto unshaken confidence in the benignity of fate, war was something remote, unimaginable, its monstrous destructions and distresses safely shut up, like the Black Death and the Great Fire, between the covers of history books. In spite of the efforts of an unusually progressive headmistress, at the school that I had just left, to interest us in the larger implications of political crises, 'current events' had remained for us unimportant precisely because they were national; they represented something that must be followed in the newspapers but would never, conceivably, have to be lived. What really mattered were not those public affairs but the absorbing incidents of our own private lives – and now, suddenly, on that summer evening, the one had relentlessly impinged upon the other, and public events and private lives had become inseparable.

For four calamitous years, with every newspaper, with every ominous telegram, with every startling ring of the telephone bell, that inescapable identity of man and the state in the modern world was forced upon our reluctant consciousness. After the war, some of us remembered that stern lesson in social responsibility for five years, some for ten; Today a few, but only a few, remember it still. Most of us, apparently, do not even trouble to pass on our knowledge to our young successors.

How many schools, in this fourteenth post-war year, have yet begun to teach their pupils that political crises affect domestic conditions? How many give lessons in current events at all? Only a few days ago a correspondence, started by a 'Worried Father' who protested that his daughter knew nothing of the world she lived in, raged in the columns of a daily paper on this very subject, and though a few girls acquitted their schools of negligence, the greater number complained that no effort had been made to keep them in touch with contemporary history. Some of them seemed blankly unaware that their elders were still dealing – or rather, failing miserably to deal – with the results of that bygone catastrophe which many people now feel that they need not remember.

Eight years ago, after making a tour of the occupied areas of Germany – the Ruhr, the Rhineland, the Saar Valley – I first began to suspect that my generation would not be able to contribute very much to the rebuilding of civilization, for the simple reason that the results of the war would last longer than ourselves. Today I know – as authoritative economists such as Sir Arthur Salter and Mr G.D.H. Cole are continually making clear to those who trouble to read them – that a heavy burden of reconstruction will lie upon the shoulders of our children; and yet, it seems, we are keeping secret from them the alien kingdom of our memories, and failing to endow them, when their day comes, with a greater power to control political and economic forces than is possible for a bankrupt and shattered generation.

For this reason I hope that we shall not cease to commemorate the Armistice; it is one of the few simple, comprehensible institutions which periodically remind us that between public events and private histories lies a close and profound relationship which we dare not forget.

DIARY EXTRACT

SUMMER 1933

In July 1933, Vera, accompanied by George Catlin and Winifred Holtby, took a holiday in northern France. She had completed her revision of Testament of Youth in March, and the book would be published by Gollancz at the end of August. Based at Hardelot-Plage, eight miles from Etaples, she explored the surrounding countryside as far south as the Somme. This was the first time Vera had returned to the scene of her wartime nursing. She had resisted the temptation to revisit it while working on her book for fear that it might play tricks on her memory.

The former battlefields were transformed from the shell-torn ground that Vera had driven over on her earlier visit in 1921, and she wondered at nature's ability to repair the ravages caused by man. On 4 August, the nineteenth anniversary of the outbreak of the Great War, she again visited Roland's grave at Louvencourt, and made a trip to see the British Memorial to the Missing of the Somme at Thiepval. This vast red-brick monument, visible for miles around, had been designed by Lutyens, and inaugurated by Edward, Prince of Wales in the summer of 1932.

Sunday July 23rd Hardelot-Plage

First advt of *Testament of Youth* by Gollancz in the Observer; in small characters above the main advt (of Strachey's *Menace of Fascism*) he had put 'Ready August 28th, *Testament of Youth*'. I conclude therefore that the *Observer* note last week was the beginning of the campaign.

Came over to Hardelot-Plage. Smooth comfortable journey to Folkestone; Channel like a duck-pond; had tea on board boat & stood at prow watching us go into Boulogne; had never felt well enough or free enough to do this before. Car from Boulogne; went through St Etienne. As soon as I saw Hôtel Aviation, felt convinced that – tho' renamed and repainted – it was the hotel (mentioned in the France chapter of *T. of Y.*) at which Norah Ashford & I stopped to have lunch in September 1917 but were ousted by the Australian officer & his lady & returned to the Pré Catelan. Everything much transformed now; a promenade has been built & many elegant villas with brightly painted windows and shutters. Process of 'development' has also produced many new roads through the pine-woods & along the front. Hotel primitive but tolerably clean & meals are excellent. Lovely views of wooded country from windows; agreeable short distance from sea.

Monday July 24th

In morning Winifred & I walked in pine-woods to try to discover the road by which I came here from Etaples, but new roads & erection of villas in woods has confused everything. In hotel salon last night a young Frenchman asked me to dance; couldn't speak English but danced beautifully; wondered if his father or elder brothers were in the War.

Sunbathed & slept on shore after lunch; after tea returned there & wrote article 'Sixteen Years After' for M. G. on my memory of Hardelot. We all three walked by one of the new roads to the Pré Catelan & had coffee; lovely garden but only vaguely as I remember it; thought it all much smarter & more sophisticated. Perhaps with more tables & officers and nurses about in uniform it actually was. Garden full of dahlias, roses & gladioli. Scarlet pimpernel, blue and purple borage and white campions in woods.

Tuesday July 25th
Quiet day. Cooler. Thick sea fog drifting in as far as pine-woods. Spent morning making list of points to be emphasised in *T. of Y.* for Macmillan's. In afternoon walked about misty sea shore; after tea sat on sand dunes & began specimen article for *Woman's Journal* on 'Our Belated Children'. Walk in pine-woods with G. & W. after dinner; coffee at Grand Hotel – pitch-pine, pretentious, non-national; might equally well have been at A.M.D.G. In sacred memory of six hundred thousand men of the armies of GREAT BRITAIN & IRELAND who fell in France and Belgium during the Great War 1914–1918. In this diocese lie their dead of the Battles of the Somme 1916, the Defence of Amiens 1918, & the March to Victory 1918.

The Australians improved the occasion thus:

To the Glory of God and to the memory of the soldiers of the AUSTRALIAN IMPERIAL FORCE who valiantly participated in the victorious defence of Amiens from March to August 1918, and gave their lives for the cause of Justice, Liberty and Humanity, this tablet is consecrated by the Government of the Commonwealth of Australia.

But the Americans merely put:

In memory of the officers and men of the Sixth Regiment United States Engineers who gave their lives in defence of Amiens March 1918.

It is as though they had said: 'We don't know much about the glory of God, & this liberty and justice business is all bunk, but we defended Amiens and here it is.' Gave me idea for article entitled 'Three Memorials'. Had also idea for lectures on 'War and its Aftermaths' (1921, 1924, 1933 travels) and 'Stages of Post-War Psychology'.

Friday August 4th
Nineteenth anniversary of the War. At 9.15, in the early morning sunshine of a perfect day, motored out from Amiens in direction of Louvencourt in private car hired yesterday. Chauffeur English, named Parsons, had been 29 years in France, married to French wife, served in War. Very full of information, much of it valuable. Talked French with a Cockney accent.

Road out towards battlefields rich with flowers – vivid blue flax, scabious, ragwort, meadowsweet, honeysuckle. First village Rainneville, still largely composed of old mud houses. Front line now ascertainable by presence of houses of new type; no mud huts in reconstructed area. Gas, light & water all brought to new villages. Passed through Pierregot and Rubempré. Lovely, mild agricultural country, productive & full of wheat; all over the Somme valley the French peasants were gathering the harvest. Made one understand France's hatred of Germany for ravishing her rich land. Impossible for anyone living in Somme area to forget the War. One vast open-air museum filled with memorials, but also exemplified the superb ability of nature to repair the ravages caused by man.

Came to *Louvencourt* by a different route from last time; remembered the two roads crossing, one uphill, and the thin line of elms beyond the cemetery. Had forgotten that Roland's grave is the first one comes upon when entering from the side path. Don't know why they put his age on the stone as 19 when he was really 20. Below his name & date of death is the motto of the Worcesters: 'Firm'; and below that the crest of the Worcesters surrounded by the words 'Honi soit qui mal y pense'. Next to him Lt. Jordan and next to Jordan Capt. Rolleston, who died of appendicitis in the summer of 1915. The cemetery is both English and French; the English are all in the middle and the French run round the inside of the encircling wall. The cemetery has both a memorial cross and a flat cenotaph with 'Their name liveth for evermore'. The path between the graves is paved and the grass very closely mown, giving an impression – as I said in *T. of Y.* – of suave velvet lawn.

On Roland's grave a pink rambler rose was growing, and a green plant with small yellow buds which I did not recognize. Picked a rambler rose for Mrs Leighton, and also a piece of rosemary from the grave of the French soldier which faces his, Pierre François Le Mer. Put on his grave, against the words 'Never Goodbye' just under the edge of the grass, the two withered roses – pink from the Leightons' garden, red from mine – that I brought from London.

All around the cemetery the harvest was being gathered into sheaves, and the air was filled with the smell of mown grass and hay. Just over the wall of the cemetery, saffron and tortoiseshell butterflies flitted over a field of purple vetch. In the cemetery is also a Jewish grave, marked with the Jewish sign, to a soldier named Baum.

We left the cemetery & drove on; I did not see, this time, the chateau that was the Casualty Clearing Station where he died. We went on to *Hédauville*, which I remember as a bumpy, shattered road full of shell holes & ruined houses, as it was a place for stores & reinforcements and was heavily shelled. Then it was marked with a placard; now the name is painted in black on a wall & a barn. The road is now smooth & smiling; I remember going down the hill and turning the corner with a bump at the bottom; this time we went so smooth & swiftly that I was only just aware of 'the long white road that ribboned down the hill'.

Passed *Mailly-Maillet* – first Somme village wh. was in front line; all new houses. Was just behind front line all through War. The great part of the Church – built by the Spaniards after the Franco-Spanish War – was left standing in spite of various bombardments; the back was shelled to pieces and the joint between the old decorated front and the rebuilt back is very obvious. Some ruined houses, never rebuilt. Chauffeur told us that after War those whose houses were ruined were promised an equivalent sum of money by the State; did not get it immediately but were given an I.O.U. Went to dealers & moneylenders (who gambled on alteration of exchanges, value of franc, etc.) and changed the I.O.U. for cash down, with which they cleared off to towns & never rebuilt their houses at all – hence ruins still left standing. Children grew up in towns & refused to return to country to work on farms.

Devastated areas

These were not rebuilt by French – who would not go into these areas because of lack of gas & water & general discomfort & sentiment – but by Italian & Spanish labourers who were encouraged to come by the French. Millions of pounds were to be earned here and they could get more than in their own countries. The French (Parsons said) also encouraged the coming of hundreds of domestic servants from Russia, as French would not work as servants in these areas. French employers paid fare of Russians & kept back the amount out of their wages. Semi-official arrangement; agency in Amiens. Many Russians stayed on after year's contract, making much better terms for themselves than the first arrangement. Very hard-working at first. Many Italian & Spanish workers have settled on their own in these areas as builders etc. French welcomed them, as people who had drifted to towns during War through losing their homes refused to go back to country. Many Belgian farmers and Flemish workers also in these areas.

Beaumont-Hamel

Stopped here to visit 'Newfoundland Park', the Newfoundland Memorial, crowned by a baying stag, in which the ground has deliberately been preserved as it was during the War – trenches, shelters, dug-outs etc.; now all in a condition of self-conscious dilapidation. At highest point was a wall with arrows pointing in direction of various important points; one said 'Newfoundland, 2600 miles'. Ground was that over which Newfoundlanders marched on July 1st, 1916; bought by Newfd & Memorial was opened by Haig in 1925.

Struck by extent by which the Dominions had taken possession of Somme region, as though they had fought all the battles. No large British memorial except that to the Missing at Thiepval Ridge.

Valley of the Ancre

To reach Thiepval Ridge from Beaumont-Hamel we had to cross the Ancre Valley, where 35,000 men were killed, wounded and drowned in three months' fighting of 1916. The valley is verdant now with meadowsweet and poppies and wheat, and the trees – almost alone in the Somme area – are the same as in 1913; the shells which passed between the ridges nearly all went over their heads. Each October when the beet-harvest is over, they still find 5 bodies a week in this valley, and the British War cemetery at Le Sars is being kept open for another two years to give them refuge.

Thiepval Ridge

On the left of the road as it reaches the top of the ridge is the Ulster Memorial to the 36th Ulster division. It looked rather too much of a pleasure park for souvenir hunters to suit my taste in memorials. The tower, which is a copy of Helen's tower near Belfast (where the Blarney Stone is – I suppose the whole thing representing the quintessence of the country for which they fought), has nothing about it to suggest War or death, but is more like an enormous water tower. The trees which line the path were planted by famous men & generals – one being Sir Henry Wilson. Close by are the Connaught and Mills Rd cemeteries – mostly Irish.

Thiepval memorial

Thiepval is the only village in France not yet built up; there were 240 people there before the War. The new Church is just begun; after the foundations were dug and the building was in progress, eight German bodies were discovered beside it. They are still there but will later be moved into a cemetery.

Great Memorial to 'The Missing of the Somme'
Unveiled on Aug. 2nd last year by the Prince of Wales. Thiepval Ridge during the Battle of the Somme was held by the Germans & dominated the whole of the British positions.

Upon the arch, inside and all around it, are inscribed the 73,367 names of those who fell on the Somme and whose bodies were never found or never identified. It made me realise what a comparatively few of the dead must have been found and buried beneath dignified tombstones inscribed with their names, for there appeared to be numbers of these memorials to the missing; I read in the *Daily Herald* that there are over 35,000 names on the one at Arras. I don't think this fact has ever been made public – or at any rate, ever emphasised.

Beside the names of the Thiepval Memorial the inscription runs as follows: 'Here are recorded names of officers and men of the British armies who fell on the Somme battlefields July 1915 to February 1918 but to whom the fortune of war denied the known and honoured burial given to their comrades in death'. I was interested especially in one name that I noticed under the heading Royal Naval Volunteer Reserve: 'Doyle, W. Served as W. Higgins'. Was Doyle, alias Higgins, a convict, I wonder, or just a boy who ran away from home?

Around the arch are also inscribed the names of the chief battle places on the Somme – Miraumont, Bapaume, Morval, Thiepval etc. In the middle below the arch is a flat cenotaph with the usual inscription: 'Their name liveth for evermore.' Below the memorial sloping downwards towards the Ancre is a cemetery where British and French are buried; hence Thiepval Ridge is the only British memorial in France with a French cemetery in front. The British graves are marked by the usual stones, the French by crosses. The cemetery was full of roses, pansies and lavender.

When we left the car I walked up the wide mown space of grass before the memorial, between flower-beds planted with violas and red roses, and stood below the immense arch of this brown & white stone memorial. Everywhere there was a scent of cut grass; and the larks were singing. In front of one lay the Somme country, miles upon misty miles of undulating verdant harvest land, rolling in its gentle curves towards the blue-grey horizon beyond which lay the spires of Amiens. And I thought what a cheating and a camouflage it all is, this combined effort of man and nature to give once more the impression that war is noble and glorious, just because its aftermath can be given an appearance of dignity and beauty after fifteen years. I never had before so clear an impression of the scene of Edward's Battle on July 1st.

The caretakers of these memorials must live a very strange, isolated life, in dug-outs, shelters and log-cabins.

Aveluy Wood
On the way from Thiepval to Albert we passed, in the near distance, Aveluy Wood, which was fought over in 1918 (mentioned

in one of Edward's letters at that time). The original trees were all shattered but the undergrowth has now grown up sufficiently to create the distant impression of a wood. But between these new trees were sinister rust-red gaps of earth where trees grew only sparsely or not at all – and these seemed to me perhaps the most significant thing that I saw, for the chauffeur told us that their redness & their barrenness was due to the explosion here of gas shells, which chemically changed the quality of the ground. Comparatively few gas shells were used in the Great War, but where they fell mark the only places where the inexhaustible capacity of Nature to repair its ravages has failed to operate. It reminded me that after the next War there will be no one left to put up memorials to the missing, for we shall all be missing – a putrefying heap of pulped flesh and poisoned blood & disintegrating bones as soon as the raiding aeroplanes have passed over us.

Just before reaching Albert we passed the famous Crucifix Corner of the Somme battlefield. On July 1st it was a big German fortified position in a stone quarry; innumerable lives were lost here and it was one of the most terrible places of that day.

Aveluy is now rebuilt – new red-brick houses, white mortar, bright blue painted railings.

Albert

Just as clock was striking 12 we ran into Albert, which I remember in 1921 as a humped ruin of stones and dust, with a few huts of reconstruction workers dotted here and there. Now a clean, bright, new town, though considerably smaller than the original, which was, our chauffeur said, the Coventry of France, and made bicycles and machinery. Now makes aeroplanes at the factory of Potez – one of the best in northern France, which employs workers from all parts. A civilian works under State control, where the men are known by numbers, not by names. A new machine works also employs all the working classes of Albert and many from Amiens.

On the site of the old shattered Basilica the new one has been built by the State; it is an exact copy of the old, which was only finished in 1900. In the midday sun it seemed to shine with its bright new paint, and the gold Virgin holding up her Child, as before, to look in the direction of the Albert–Bapaume road, gleamed in the sun. As we went past, the chimes were sounding for midday on the 19th anniversary of the War. Town has been adopted by Birmingham, and Birmingham presented a clock which was striking 12 from the tall tower of the new town hall surrounded by a French flag flying half-mast (the only flag we saw that day to suggest that anyone remembered it was a war anniversary). The chimes, we were told, are an exact replica of those of Big Ben.

As we ran into Albert the chauffeur told us the true story of the Virgin of the Basilica. One legend used to say that when she finally fell the War would end; another that as long as the statue remained on the steeple the French would never lose Albert and that it actually fell as the Germans entered the town (this latter repeated in *T. of Y.*). What actually happened was that after the Germans took the town in 1918 they used the Basilica as an observation post as it gave a marvellous view of the entire enemy forces. We ourselves therefore shot down the steeple (chauffeur says he was with the Captain who gave the order to fire at it), and the Virgin fell, was smashed to pieces on the pavement, and the fragments carried away by the Germans as souvenirs.

We lunched at the somewhat optimistically named Hôtel de la Paix, where the proprietor is an Italian who fought on the Italian front during the War, & afterwards worked as a waiter on the Riviera & at Vittel.

Road from Albert to Bapaume
Not far out of Albert we passed the craters of La Boiselle, which I remember seeing in 1921, in the midst of a completely devastated region. The craters (the biggest of which was used as German Headquarters in 1918) are now becoming grown-over with coarse grass & all gradually (though very slowly) filling up as the earth silts down into them in rainy seasons. Homely hens now peck peacefully around them and placid cows crop the rough grass at the edge. The chauffeur pointed out the hump of earth ¾ mile back where the shaft was let down for the tunnel to the mine; it was started three months before July 1st and made by coal-miners from Northumberland and Durham. This was the first time that mine craters (a method afterwards 'perfected' at Messines Ridge) were used as an offensive measure in the War. The chief regiments at La Boiselle were the Irish and Scottish Tynesiders (Tyneside Scottish, 34th Division), mostly composed of employees of the Newcastle Docks. On the opposite side of the road to Bapaume is a memorial to these two regiments, on which the inscription concludes: 'Think not that the struggle and the sacrifice were in vain.' Here the old German

front line ran through the village cemetery – now completely demolished.

Pozières

At Pozières is a huge cemetery, walled and colonnaded, where are 2770 graves and, carved between the pillars, the names of 14,690 'missing'. (? What has become of all these bodily remnants? Are they collected together in huge common graves, or have they been exploded, ploughed & steam-rollered into the soil, & are we driving over them all the time? No wonder the French do not care to live in this deceptively beautiful but gruesome charnel house of a region.)

In front of the cemetery was an Australian memorial, marked with the Rising Sun (the Australians captured Pozières, & the big cemetery was started by them to hold the first Australian dead). The new red-roofed mayor's house and school [were] built out of penny subscriptions from the children of Melbourne.

The Canadians first came into action on Pozières Ridge. Here too is the Tanks Corps memorial, on the first place where tanks were used; it includes a model of the four different kinds of tanks used in the War & the chains encircling it came also from tank wheels.

On the right of Pozières is Martinpuich, where is High Wood (also containing a memorial to the 47th London Division, which lost 3000 men in 24 hours when first in action). They captured it on September 16th, 1916, with the aid of tanks. Here, between High Wood and Le Sars, the first battle of the Somme ended. The 47th Division was chiefly composed of employees of the General Omnibus Company.

Canadian Memorial at Courcelette

Massed with pink ramblers and surrounded by maples, grown from seeds sent over from Canada. The only trees in France that change colour in autumn.

Bapaume

Now all rebuilt with big station and large market. Like other towns rebuilt since War is now complete with gas, water & electricity, which comes mostly from Bethune – hence the pylons across the Somme country. Chauffeur told us that everywhere the roads are being widened because huge 3-ton motor lorries hurtle down them 3 abreast during the night. Thought Bapaume rather a messy mixture of old & new. Did not stop.

Mont St Quentin

Hill captured by Australians who struggled through marshes below dressed only in shorts and shirts, and took it with the bayonet. (River Somme flows through plain beyond marshes.) Horrible memorial on road up hill, showing statue of Australian pushing his bayonet into a recumbent German eagle. Memorial is to the 2nd Australian Division.

Péronne

Big new town with modern hospital. Always very difficult to take because so largely surrounded by water & marshland. Nevertheless, was taken in both 1870 & 1914. Stopped in market square; went into chief Hôtel St Claude (rebuilt in both 1870 & 1914) & bought postcards. Large place, much bigger than Bapaume, and has not a particularly new appearance as many of the old bricks were used in the rebuilding. One café marked as having been burnt by the Germans in both 1870 & 1917. Also a large shop (millinery and miscellaneous haber-dashery) inscribed: 'Built 1792. Destroyed 1870 & 1916. Rebuilt 1873 & 1924.' Though the whole town was destroyed, it gives the impression of having been there for decades. After War adopted by Blackburn, which built the new Blackburn Bridge over the Somme Canal. (Some of these reconstructed towns don't have such a bad time &, if one can forget the dead, must be much more convenient to live in than the older ones.)

La Chapelette

On main road to Amiens, beyond Péronne. Indian soldiers first came into action here 1916. Indian cemetery similar to ours but no crosses on stone. Massed with pink roses.

We were now on 'the great road from Amiens to St Quentin', along which the Germans both advanced & retreated in 1918. Was in French hands for greater part of the War. All flat rolling country like Yorkshire Wolds; harvest everywhere. French cemetery at Villers Carbonnel. French (and occasional Americans) spoil appearance of cemeteries by taking their dead out of them and removing them home. British not allowed to do this.

Proyart

Passed this village close to which is Big Bertha that shelled Amiens (in valley at Chuignes) . Passed Heath cemetery and the so-called 'Mysterious house', which though four times in the front line was never destroyed because no one was sure to whom it belonged (*i.e.*, who was in occupation of the cellars), but after War all the apparatus there was found to be German.

Valley of Death

Passed through here beyond Proyart. So-called because full of British gun positions which were constantly shelled; also lorries of stores or reinforcements were forced to mount slowly road going up from valley on either side, & so were constantly shelled and hit.

Americans in action

Passed wood of Le Hamel where Americans were first in action on Somme, July 4th, 1918. Germans found here chained to guns. (First American attack in War made at St Michel in 1918.)

Villers-Bretonneux

Virtually a suburb of Amiens; last village Germans reached in 1918 – got just beyond it to l'Abbé Wood. Australians held the line from here through Corbie and Bray. Adopted by Melbourne & Victoria. A *rosierie* here (rose garden) & old ruined chateau. French funeral taking place in local cemetery. Passed also one of the 383 stones put up along 450 miles from the coast to the Vosges to commemorate the position of the front line. German front line (two black marks across road) just beside it. Stone marked: 'Ici fut repoussé l'envahisseur 1918.'

L'Abbé Wood

Germans reached here in the March–April offensive 1918, & were pushed back to where stone was. Here Adelaide cemetery – only one where all the dead were killed in 1918. No original trees – only undergrowth – in wood. Marvellous straight road – in front the gradually looming view of Amiens impressed me more than anything throughout the journey except the view from Thiepval Ridge, for it made me realise what the Germans must have felt as they came in sight of what must have been the largest town in France that they had the chance to take during the War. It must have seemed so near, so accessible, yet they never took it. The Cathedral, built in a hollow so that it recedes as you get near the town, yet so high that it dominates the whole countryside from a distance, must have been very easy to shell completely, yet they never destroyed it. Why? Did they mean to make the town their headquarters in final victorious campaign of War, & use Cathedral for observation? We ourselves used it in 1918 as observation post on German positions – advantage given us so great that this was a main reason why the Germans wanted to capture Amiens.

Back at hotel with half an hour to spare before train; wrote hasty letters to Mrs Leighton (enclosing rambler & rosemary) and Beverley Nichols whose *Cry Havoc!* I had carried with me all over the Somme battlefield. V. hot train back to Boulogne. Missed bus so drove back to Hardelot in car at sunset through roads scented with smell of mown hay.

Saturday August 5th
Started writing articles about battlefields. Very interesting letter in afternoon from Ernest Raymond about *T. of Y.* – he had got to p. 241, just after Roland's death, & couldn't stop thinking about it. Lost part of my *Clarion* article owing to wind on verandah; very much annoyed. Perfect night; orange moon.

Sunday August 6th
Finished & typed articles which I hope may be accepted by *Week-end Review* and *Clarion* & sent them off. Very hot – 92° in London; must have been quite that here. Walked to tea at Pré Catelan over burning road. Entire population of Hardelot seemed to be talking & drinking round hotel so we walked after dinner to Golfer's Hotel for coffee, & back. Lovely scented walk through pine-woods under full moon.

Monday August 7th
Most perfect day since we came – hot but not tiring; constant gentle breeze. Spent whole day on sea shore, bathing, sun-bathing, reading *Cry Havoc!* and walking. V.S.J. went off with her French count, so after tea W. & I walked across sands about 2½ miles to next village in direction of Boulogne. Real country fishing village, full of smells of drains & fish. Back over perfect sands in pearly light.

Wednesday August 9th
Typed review & wrote letters. W. had one of her headaches & felt inactive, so V.S.J. & I had tea at Golfer's Hotel & walked on to

the old chateau. Entrance now closed by wire as castle is supposed to be dangerous but we got under the fence & looked in. Inside ceilings all falling in, but outside seems likely to last for the present though topmost (red) turret looks very drunk. Huge cracks in walls & steps. 'Gaudeam adfero' written over doorway a strange comment on situation. Garden which must once have been an exquisite dream now a wild tangle of grass, thistles & brambles below trees, which though dusty & dilapidated are still magnificent – ilex, alder, elms, walnut, poplars. Very much 'they say the lion & the lizard keep . . .'. Shouldn't like to be here at twilight – feel sure it is full of owls. A workman was inside the grounds mending his cart; V.S.J. asked him questions about the chateau & it turned out that his mother had been a servant there. Some years before the War it belonged to a Miss Guy or Gye – one of an English family all brought up there; then it became a restaurant, & during the War was commandeered for the Army & used as an instruction school ('Sports Shed' still written on one of the outhouses). Probably during War garden went to rack and ruin (one pink rose bush & a clump of goldenrod seem to be all that is left of it) and whole place was neglected, so that no one would take it on & spend money on it, & it is now rapidly becoming a ruin. Until a year or two ago Miss Guy wrote to the workman's mother regularly & always inquired after the castle. A year or two ago she came back to see it – and was evidently so much horrified at what she saw that ever since she has not written, or been heard of here.

Walked out along old carriage drive; ancient gates were firmly shut behind us by a lodge-keeper's wife. Walked back past mere (many fishers) and golf course; mere almost violently blue, & divine light on distant sandhills. Walked up old road to Etaples opposite Pré Catelan & came out on to big new white road to Le Touquet.

Thursday August 10th
Spent most of day drafting, on & off, 1600 word article for *Daily Telegraph* on 'What Shall I Do If My Son Wants to Join the OTC?' By afternoon mail, gorgeous letter from Frank Swinnerton (to whom Odette sent a copy) about my book; says he has written the greater part of his literary letter to the *Chicago Tribune* about it, & Gollancz can quote from this if he likes. Also an engagement from Christy for lecture to Leeds Luncheon Club, Jan. 25th, on 'Should Autobiographies Be Forbidden?' Dined at Pré Catelan as it was V.S.J.'s last evening; also had had enough of French families for the present.

Saturday August 12th
Went over country by bus to see Etaples & Camiers. Lovely day; strong breeze, bright blue sky and clouds. Had long wait at Condette; ordered black coffee in roadside café where 3 French workmen (typical *poilus*) were drinking beer and *café au rhum*. All very gay and loquacious. Were shortly joined by a fourth from the wine-merchant's van. Among the bottles ordered were two empty ones, but this form of 'try on' appeared to disturb and deceive no one. Man merely remarked philosophically 'C'est la vie' (evidently the French equivalent to: 'It came away in me 'and') and was invited by the vivacious young woman at

the bar to sit down and have a drink with the other three, which he did.

We got off the bus at Camiers and walked towards Etaples along the once familiar road. We went into the churchyard at Camiers where we found the economical inhabitants had made the 1870 war memorial 'Aux enfants de Camiers mort pour la patrie' do again by simply adding the words '1914–1918' under '1870'. Of the old-fashioned, rather ornate and pointed type, it was in curious contrast to the bare, simple-formed memorials in most of the villages and cemeteries.

Then we walked along the path beside the mere just below the railway line to the 'Manor House', which during the War was a restaurant where Faith & I had so many large & satisfying teas. It is still blue-painted, but is now a laundry, which looks somewhat dejected, & all the clamorous ducks and chickens have vanished. Then we walked between pine-woods and sandhills along the straight, switchback road to Etaples. In one place mounds of earth had grown over piles of old petrol tins; all along the left-hand side where camps had been was coarse grass and ragwort, toadflax, mustard and bugloss. I picked a piece of toadflax from the side of 'the road to Camiers', and later a sprig of bugloss from where 24 General had been.

At Etaples cemetery we stopped for an hour. In contrast to the small cemeteries on the Somme it looked enormous, spreading like a huge open fan from the pine-woods on the top of the hill down the slope to the flat, marshy ground which surrounds the railway line. The graves must run into thousands and it is surely still the largest military cemetery in France. It was difficult in so enormous a place to tell just how the graves were arranged, but most of the officers appear to be together in the rows which start at the foot of the cenotaph and extend in lines of about twenty to the railway line. Among them was one VAD and one or two Sisters – those killed in the Canadian hospital during the great air raid of May 19th, 1918. One – a certain Sister K. Macdonald who was evidently slain by a bomb while actually on duty – was described on the headstone as 'killed in action'. Above her name was the maple leaf, which is I suppose the emblem of the Canadian nursing service. The VAD – named, I think, Hallam – was described as 'Nursing Member, Voluntary Aid Detachment', and had above her name the combined emblem of the BRCS and Order of St John. I looked for the grave of my Corporal Smith – who died on Dec. 27th, 1917 in my ward and was apparently a vicar's son, which would account for his charming manners – but though I got the number from the register, I could not find it.

The German graves still have on them the original grey crosses (presumably the German Govt can't yet afford stones – I wonder where all the German cemeteries are) now very weather-beaten and many marked 'Unknown German Soldier' – which seems curious; one wonders how men who died of wounds in hospital could be quite unknown. A few of these German graves (which just like the rest were richly decked with the magnificent summer flowers that filled the whole cemetery) were among the British, but most of them were away at the side nearest Camiers, together with the graves of Indians and other natives – 'all the outcasts together', as Winifred described them, though the Indians of course had headstones. These were inscribed 'Here is Honoured . . .' and then the name. The Portuguese were also buried among the British; they too have only the original wooden crosses but these have been painted white to resemble the headstones of those who are 'honoured'.

In one little corner on the right of the memorial stone (as one stood with one's back to the sea) was a tiny piece of cemetery surrounding a solitary Chinese grave, with the name inscribed in Chinese characters; it was that of a member of the Chinese Labour Corps and below the name were inscribed in English the words: 'A good reputation endureth for ever.' His number also in the Labour Corps was given in English characters, and the flowers and tiny hedge round the grave were arranged in a Chinese pattern. Beyond him, still further in a corner – were they perhaps unconsecrated? – were about a dozen graves of other 'natives' – West Indian and S. African.

Before going round the graves we sat for some time on the steps leading down to the cemetery and looked at the registers of graves from the two closets in the ashlar wall. I recognised one or two that I remember of men whom I had nursed or heard of. But still more interesting were some of the inscriptions and the marks in the Visitors' Book for 1933 which was enclosed with the registers. Winifred and I wrote our names with the date in it thus: 'Vera Brittain, 19 Glebe Place, London SW3. Nursed as a VAD at 24 General Hospital, Etaples, 1917–1918.' 'Winifred Holtby, QMAAC, Camiers, 1918.' And below our names I wrote the words: 'No More War!'

Afterwards I copied down some of the mostly impressive remarks, which were as follows: 1) Pierre Luick – no date & no address but simply the words: 'Et cela confirme mon opinion bas la guerre.' 2) No signature, but marked 'Du Havre, 28.7.33.' 'Parmi nos amusements, nous n'oublions pas ceux qui sont morts pour nous et souhaitons que leur exemple serve aux vivants pour ne jamais revoir ces calamités.' 3) Marked: 'Lefevre, Calais. Saisons, Calais.' '"Le profit personnel est responsable de la guerre. Seul le proletariat peut hitter contre la guerre. Proletaires de tous les pays unissez-vous." (Karl Marx).' 4) Marked only 'Gaby.' 'Que ces anglais reposent en paix pour l'éternité. Amen.' 5) 'G.P. Symonds, Hon. CF Who buried many of those whose bodies lie here. Aug. 9th 1933. Well done, gardeners!' 6) Anonymous: 'Que tous les peuples prennent exemple. Les Anglais, Portugais, Canadiens, Indiens, Allemands, tous sont unis dans une paix éternelle. Puissent-ils tous reposer en paix.' And finally, 7) '5 Réfugiés allemands, 10.8.33.'

We left the cemetery at last and walked on to Etaples, down the road where 24 General was, and the humped, ragwort-covered earth where the huts were is marked everywhere 'Danger. Défense d'entrer.' I looked across the wide tumbled field to the distant trees beneath which was once the German ward. It was all very queer that it should be so quiet and still, when I remembered it so full of hurry and anxiety, apprehension and pain. To the right was a clear, beautiful view of Le Touquet, now unobstructed by huts; above the woods appeared the roof of the Royal Picardy, whose top windows must look straight on to Etaples cemetery. I wonder how many of the wealthy people who stay there ever notice it, or remember.

Sunday August 13th

Finished & sent on *D. Telegraph* article on OTC As usual Sunday concourse was round hotel, W. & I took our lunch out and picnicked in the pine-woods beyond the Pré Catelan. Sat in lovely dappled sunlight & shadows on carpet of pine-needles; gorgeous scent of pine-needles everywhere. W. stung by wasp on way, but we got ammonia at once from grocer & no apparent harm resulted. Stayed in wood till nearly 4.0; sounds of distant thunder sent us back but no storm happened, only a few drops of rain. Walked up & down shore after tea, watching lovely children playing on beach. Gorgeous sunset. Drafted two more articles for M. *Guardian.* Press cutting from *Newsagent & Booksellers' Review* saying that *T. of Y.* looks like being another 'winner'.

ILLUSION ON THE SOMME

The sight of the Thiepval Memorial to the Missing of the Somme – and of the 73,367 names inscribed on it, of men from that bloody campaign whose bodies had never been found or identified – had a profound effect on Vera. Here, in one of a number of polemical articles written following her visit to the Somme, Vera considers the threat of another world conflict that may reduce civilian populations 'to putrescent heaps of rotting flesh . . . and disintegrating bones'.

———

One recent summer's day in France – a day which vividly recalled to me the little war that you've probably forgotten, since it happened so very long ago – I drove out of Amiens towards the Somme battlefields with two companions. One of these was a writer of satires on contemporary life; the other chanced, most appropriately, to be a book – the *Cry Havoc!* of Beverley Nichols.

At the hour when we left the street beside the once-threatened cathedral, where the specimen collection of war memorials and the still shattered windows smashed in the German offensive of 1918 preserve the war for our ex-allies as an event of only yesterday, the majority of worthy citizens across the Channel were still enjoying their London newspapers. And some of them that morning were doubtless edified to learn that 'there are moments in the history of a nation' (such as 4 August 1914) 'when decisions are reached by instinct rather than by calculation and reasoning'.

In my early youth I was often told that women were an inferior species because they based their actions on instinct instead of upon reason. But apparently this quality, so deplorable in the case of females, becomes admirable – for reasons which are not quite clear to me – as soon as it characterizes a whole people; for a little further down in the column, the leader-writer concluded that 'the nation . . . has never had cause to repent its resolution'.

Except in the most accessible French towns, the larger London newspapers are not available on the day of publication, so I had not this inspiring thought to console me as I stood on Thiepval Ridge beneath the arch of the great memorial to the missing of the Somme, and looked across the now verdant slopes of the River Ancre to the reconstructed village of Beaumont Hamel.

It was a perfect summer day; all over the undulating miles of the Somme valley, rolling away into the blue-grey distance which hid the spires of Amiens, the French peasants were gathering the harvest. 'No cause to repent' – since the blood which once watered those fields and the flesh that manured them have apparently created a richer dust for the satisfaction of the spring sowers. I wonder whether the mothers and wives and sisters and sweethearts of the 73,367 undiscovered or unidentified men whose names are inscribed on the Thiepval memorial would accept that statement? And whether we, to whom all but one or two of them were strangers, have no reason to regret that they are not with us, to raise the standard of our literature, our art, our science, our struggling, floundering politics?

Is there, finally, no cause for repentance in the manner of their deaths – those agonizing mutilations, those grotesque defacements which left nothing but a shattered arm, an isolated leg, the obscene remnants of a detached human skull, to indicate that here was one of those young men who composed what Mr Hugh Dalton, in a House of Commons speech quoted by Beverley Nichols, described as 'the morning glory that was the flower of Anzac, the youth of Australia and New Zealand, yes, and the youth of our own country'? That horror of utter, humiliating annihilation cannot be concealed even by the lofty inscription carved so gracefully upon the memorial:

Here are recorded names of officers and men of the British Armies who fell on the Somme Battlefields, July, 1915, to February, 1918, but to whom the fortune of War denied the known and honoured burial given to their comrades in death.

Grave and beautiful words, you say, which bring tears to the eyes and a sob to the throat? Yes, no doubt – but let's have the truth. They are all a cheating and a camouflage, these noble memorials, with their mown, scented lawns, these peaceful cemeteries filled with red roses and purple pansies, these harvest fields which help to create the illusion that war is a glorious thing because so much of its aftermath can be rendered lovely and dignified. They do not compensate the young men for the lives that they laid down, and they do not recompense you and me for having to go through the long years without them.

I am glad that I carried Beverley Nichols' book with me through Hédauville and Thiepval, and to Albert, with its shining rebuilt basilica, and to La Boiselle, where the homely hens peck on the edges of the mine-craters, and to Pozières, with its Australian monument, and to Bapaume, with its modern, labour-saving houses, and to Péronne, which now flourishes exceedingly as the post-war godchild of Blackburn. I am glad because his book assisted me to remain undeluded by those beautiful memorial acres, for it reminded me that the Somme battle need never have been fought at all. 'Germany,' he states, 'would have capitulated in 1915, its ironmasters have since admitted, if Briey had been bombarded.' For Briey, so Mr Nichols tells us, was the region which furnished the material for the guns that slaughtered the French and British troops, and through the influence of the great metallurgical industry it remained immune from Allied attack all through the war.

This sinister jewel of information brings me, along with the author of *Cry Havoc!* to another theme which may, if we reflect upon it, give all of us sufficient cause for repentance before we are done. If Beverley Nichols and his instructors – the expert contributors to *What Would be the Character of a New War?* and the writers of that admirable UDC pamphlet, 'The Secret International' – are not deceiving us, there will be no dignified memorials after the next war to end war, and no one to put them up. In that war we shall all be the missing – you and I and editorial leader-writers and our small sons and daughters who now play their games with such happy confidence in the world that politicians and generals and armament manufacturers have made for them. Far more expeditiously than the missing of the Somme we shall be reduced by air attacks and gas shells to putrescent heaps of rotting flesh and poisoned blood and disintegrating bones.

But such a remote contingency, you say – you who live so comfortably in King's Lynn or Truro or Cheltenham. Let me assure you that these things are not nightmares but strong probabilities, and once war breaks out again they will turn into certainties. If you don't believe me, read Beverley Nichols – or, if you have a scientific turn of mind, tackle What *Would be the Character of a New War?* itself. And if these still fail to convince you, take a car from Amiens on your next holiday and visit Aveluy Wood.

Comparatively few gas shells were used in the last war, but where they fell Nature has alone been unable to repair the hideous wrongs wrought upon her hills and fields. Aveluy Wood is one of the 'beauty spots' in which they were used, and in the midst of it are treeless spaces where the chemically changed earth has turned rust-red. Stand, as I did, upon the road from Amiens to Albert, and look at those acres where, even in the elementary days of gas, resistant Nature was so transformed that fifteen years afterwards she still preserves the illusion of spilt blood. And I don't think, even if you do live in Cheltenham or Harrogate, that you'll feel altogether happy about that next war.

Vera, with nursing sister, at the bedside of a patient.
1st London General, Camberwell, 1915

WHAT NURSING TAUGHT ME

Vera's reminiscences, from 1950, of her experiences as a VAD in the First World War, contrasting them with the far more limited opportunities for volunteer nursing overseas in the Second World War, which had ended five years earlier.

––––––––

During the First World War, which the crowded and violent age we live in has now caused to seem so remote, I spent four years as a VAD nurse in a variety of hospitals both at home and abroad Of the six in which I served, four were military hospitals under the control of the War Office, and two were independent civilian hospitals, one in London and one in the provinces.

I am not sure whether military service can justifiably be described as 'national service' in a contemporary sense. But whether or not the two are comparable, I found the 'national service' of those days infinitely preferable to the four months spent under the auspices of voluntary civilian institutions, with the endless series of special traditions and nagging restrictions.

It seems strange that the uncongenial tasks reluctantly assumed so long ago in the name of patriotism should still have their value after thirty years. Such a consequence of 'active service' was certainly one that I never expected. As a student who had just gone up to Oxford with an exhibition in English Literature, which was the more treasured because it had been worked for and won in the teeth of family opposition, I already cherished private ambitions of becoming a writer. Nursing was definitely the last form of occupation that I should ever have chosen. I had hardly been conscious that nurses existed until the outbreak of war gave them a new and important national status.

The duties assigned to a raw hospital recruit periodically filled me with a boredom and loathing so acute that I dreaded the coming of each new day. This unconstructive attitude persisted until my work took me overseas, first to the Mediterranean and then to the Western Front, and brought me the thrill of unknown lands and vivid new scenes to mitigate the day-by-day routine of cleaning, bed-making, dressings, and bowl-washing.

The young volunteer nurses of the First World War were actually more fortunate in the knowledge that they acquired than their successors of the Second. Even during the height of 1940–41 air raids, casualties (at any rate in England) never came so fast as the casualties caused by such great holocausts as the first Battle of the Somme in 1916, the Battle of Passchendaele in 1917 and the Battle of Amiens (the last great German offensive) in the spring of 1918.

Catastrophic as those casualties were from every other standpoint, they brought to the 'untrained' volunteers an experience of surgical nursing which seldom comes even to the trained civilian specialist. With a competence learned in the hard school of experience, the young VADs tackled fractures, haemorrhages, and the dressing of amputations on a scale which the insufficiency of trained Sisters made unavoidable. A young woman who comes on duty one morning, as I did in March, 1918, to find herself in sole charge of forty desperately wounded men of whom at least a quarter need emergency operations, tends ever afterwards to discount the fearsomeness of exacting but less nerve-racking experiences.

The amount of foreign service available, with all its colour and informality, to volunteer nurses between 1914 and 1919 was also far greater than that which offered itself between 1939 and 1945. The speed with which the Nazis overran almost the whole continent of Europe in 1940 reduced the areas of possible overseas service, and compelled most volunteers to serve in civilian hospitals temporarily adapted to the demands of Service ministries or Civil Defence.

It must have been about ten years after I was demobilized in 1919, that I first began to see my period of active hospital service as something more than a disastrous interruption to a promising literary career. In 1929 the process had barely begun by which my war experiences were eventually transformed into the substance of a book, widely read ever since its first appearance in 1933. But a decade after the war I did realize that those experiences were not misfortunes to be deplored, but spiritual lessons to be accepted with gratitude.

Because of them, I 'belonged' to my generation in a way that I could never have done if I had sat out the war in Oxford lecture-rooms. I was part of a fellowship of suffering whose members had learned in a hard school that human beings, whatever their national labels, possess an underlying unity which makes war the sin against the Holy Ghost, and the attainment of reconciliation our generation's reply to the age-long challenge of Calvary.

I had learnt other lessons too, less profound than this great spiritual truth, but more fundamental than the useful mastery of invalid cooking, and the habit of always carrying smelling-salts, an iodine-pencil, and a bandage along with my lipstick and powder-compact in my handbag in case I should find myself on the scene of an accident some valuable minutes before the arrival of doctor or nurse. One of these lessons was the importance, in one's personal life as a prelude to the service of others in sickness or distress, of learning to conquer fear.

When I first went into hospital, I was not only a natural but an ignorant coward. The modern jargon of popular psychology 'reaction', 'repression', 'anxiety neurosis', 'combat-fatigue', 'battle-hysteria' – had not then become the current coinage of speech which is sometimes more glib than intelligent. But I saw enough cases of what was then called 'shell-shock' to realize the intimate relationship between body and mind, and subsequently to understand the modern psychotherapists' insistence that more people are ill because they are miserable, than miserable because they are ill.

One dark winter evening when I was on night-duty in France, a patient had been brought into our medical ward who could neither move nor speak. Though the doctors could find no physical explanation for his condition, we were obliged to treat him as a case of total paralysis until he was sent down the line – to the care, let us hope, of some specialist better acquainted with the strange vagaries of the human mind than the army doctors at Etaples in 1917.

After that, the text-books could teach me little about the manifestations of conversion-hysteria, though I still had everything to learn about its causes. I acquired this knowledge gradually, my interest deepened by the tragic murder trial of an acquaintance who killed a much-loved wife during one of the periodic fits of amnesia which were the legacy of a bomb explosion on the Western Front. By the time I had finished thinking out the implications of that story, I had come to see fear, whether it increases the shock of an individual accident or precipitates the national hysteria which leads to war, as among the mortal enemies of mankind.

I do not remember the exact moment at which I perceived that the mind which fear can anaesthetize and paralyse has within itself the power to discipline and finally eliminate that fear, setting itself free for a life as glorious and spiritually untrammelled as the lives of the saints. 'Always do what you are afraid to do', says an old French proverb. The impulse of a born coward to immunize herself from fear by obeying the proverb, to grasp the nettle danger and out of it pluck the flower safely, dates back to that case of pseudo-paralysis brought into an army hospital in France during a Christmas season over thirty years ago.

I hope, in conclusion, that those who organize our present National Hospital Service have mastered the distinction between essentials and non-essentials which put the overseas medical camps of the First World War into a category quite different from that of its home hospitals staffed by civilians. How often I saw the bright-eyed keenness and youthful readiness to endure, which meant life and hope to wounded men at the back of the Front, dissipated in England by perpetual bullying about the details of a uniform which was anyhow out of date, and by a hidebound insistence upon greater attention to brass sterilizers and metal bed-rails than to the welfare of the patients.

Discipline must exist, of course – but self-discipline voluntarily accepted is always better than discipline dictatorially imposed from above. Some regulations are necessary to the smooth running of a hospital service, but the imparting of confidence to the sick matters more than the number of buttons on a coat, and the conquest of fear in one patient alone has higher value than a hundred newly polished sterilizers.

Above all other qualities in hospital comes the recognition of humanity – its oneness and its dignity – and the response to its needs. Nothing is harder to retain in the medical service than those human values, nothing easier to acquire than that bright immunity to pity which 'compensates' for horror and pain by a protective armour of callousness, and forgets that the most impaired patient is not merely a suffering body but potentially a triumphant spirit. The doctors and nurses who retain the consciousness of humanity at whatever personal cost will become the stars in the firmament of the National Health Service as surely as they were the lanterns of hope to the sick and wounded of two World Wars.

WAR SERVICE IN PERSPECTIVE

This essay, contributed to Promise of Greatness, *a volume commemorating the fiftieth anniversary of the Armistice in 1968, was one of the last sustained pieces of writing that Vera completed before her death in March 1970. She was the only woman included among the contributors to the book.*

Four years earlier, the BBC's landmark documentary series The Great War, *had devoted just minutes out of its twenty-six episodes to a consideration of women's experience of the 1914–18 War. It would be another decade before historical evaluation of the War's impact upon women would begin to emerge, and in this evaluation* Testament of Youth *was to play a crucial role.*

————

Since the fiftieth anniversary of the outbreak of the First World War, I have kept a pile of newspaper clippings beside me in a big folder. What do these clippings, collected from a large number of papers and magazines, emphasize from the impressions of numerous contributors?

First, I find a long section on the weapons of war, showing many varieties of protective device, from the gas masks developed out of the primitive protection of a wet handkerchief to elaborate helmets resembling a Martian face mask dreamed of in a science-fiction story by H.G. Wells. The clippings go on to give pictures of different types of shells, designs for experimental airplanes, and plans for the vulnerable zeppelins. Then come photographs of the terrifying tanks, which at first overwhelmed Britain's enemies by their strange monstrosity. Finally, by way of an anticlimax, we see pictures of London's terracotta-coloured B type buses which proved ideal for the transport of troops in France.

Another bundle of clippings is devoted to the assorted war posters by means of which truth – 'the first casualty in wartime' – gradually lost its integrity. This was achieved through the undermining of mental independence by emotional appeals which varied from representations of the Kaiser as an inventor of ingenious atrocities to the sentimental pictures of white-haired mothers urging their sons to fight. There followed a series of grotesque legends, which began with the story of the corpse factory in which the bodies of dead soldiers were said to be converted into explosives and went on to the tale of the entirely fictitious *Lusitania* Medal reported to have been struck at the Kaiser's suggestion and bestowed on the crew of the submarine which sank the *Lusitania* in 1915.

I still recall the contemporary reactions, including my own, to these crude but graphic appeals. Even in the eyes of an ingenuous girl recently out of school, most of them seemed just plain silly. Kitchener's finger pointing from numerous hoardings left me quite unmoved by its hysterical monotony. Though I was about to become a college highbrow, my responses to pressure, so untypical in most ways of the society in which I was brought up, were, I think, characteristic of the nation as a whole. Before the

Second World War the patient work of such political research workers as Arthur Ponsonby – a founder of the Union of Democratic Control and Foreign Secretary in Britain's first Labour government, whose classic *Falsehood in Wartime* was published in 1928 – had unmasked the most extravagant stories. These investigations left the British people imbued with a healthy scepticism which even the newer forms of propaganda, such as radio and television, failed to undermine. A comment made to me by a London workingwoman on the consequences of an air raid in 1944 must have been typical of many others: 'I heard it on the BBC, so it can't be true.'

From graphic examples of propaganda, my collection moves on to the numerous portraits of British war leaders – Haig, Plumer, Herbert Lawrence, William Robertson, all of whom looked well fed, substantial, and complacent. They make a gruesome contrast to the fragile wraith of bedridden Private George Oakley of the Middlesex Regiment, who enlisted at the age of eighteen and, when his picture was published, had spent forty-eight years in the Star and Garter Home for ex-servicemen at Richmond, Surrey. He was one of 28,000,000 men, wounded on both sides of the struggle, many of whom are still living a hidden death-in-life existence in servicemen's hospitals.

Other pictures show the gruesome litter of war amid the forests of black crosses in a German cemetery. One newspaper sent a special correspondent to travel round the former battle-fronts and photograph whatever items of surviving debris seemed most worthy of record after fifty years. He came back with pictures, among many other things, of bent bayonets protruding from the earth at Verdun – a reminder of the men buried alive by bombardment as they waited to go over the top.

On the slope of what was once Hill 60 the breech of a machine gun lies slowly rusting away. In a private wood near Albert in Picardy, the ground is still thick with remnants of war: helmets and old boots, barbed wire and beer bottles, which lie undisturbed amid branches and brambles where they were left by departing British soldiers half a century ago.

From the nature study of war's sombre remains, we move on to the special supplement of a historically minded editor who chose to commemorate the fiftieth anniversary of the war by pictures of the Archduke Franz Ferdinand and his family – a mild and well-intentioned man who did not deserve his fate of identification with the tragedy that sparked off four years of atrocity and mutilation. One cracked picture shows him with a brisk handlebar moustache in a bright blue uniform which seems to reflect the limpid color of the unferocious, philosophical Hapsburg eyes.

A 'family portrait' brings back to life the plain, Teutonic Duchess Sophie and the three morganatic children – the handsome Maximilian, their elder son, who was mayor of Artstetten until his death in 1962; the second son, Ernst, who was sent to Dachau for five years by the Nazis and who died after his release; and Sophie, Franz Ferdinand's only daughter, an amiable-looking *Hausfrau* who is now the Countess von Nostitz-Rieneck and lives with her husband in a small villa at Salzburg.

As though by intentional contrast, the same magazine shows a grimacing art student in Munich listening to the proclamation of war from the midst of the crowd. It is Adolf Hitler, whose words from *Mein Kampf* are quoted:

> My own attitude towards the conflict was both simple and clear. In my eyes it was not Austria fighting to get a little satisfaction out of Serbia but Germany fighting for her life, the German nation for its 'to be or not to be', its freedom and future. It would have to follow in Bismarck's footsteps; young Germany must again defend what the fathers had heroically fought for from Weissenburg to Sedan and Paris. But if the struggle was to be a victorious one, our people would by their own force take their place again among the great nations, and then the German Reich could stand as a mighty guardian of peace, without the necessity to curtail its children's daily bread for the sake of this peace.
>
> On the Third of August I addressed a petition to His Majesty King Ludwig III to be allowed to serve in a Bavarian regiment. The Cabinet Office during those days certainly had its hands pretty full, and my joy was all the greater when my petition was granted the same day.
>
> Now began for me, as for every German, the greatest and most unforgettable period of my life on earth. Compared with the events of that mighty struggle, all the past fell into empty oblivion. I think with pride and sorrow of those days and back to the weeks of the beginning of our nation's heroic fight, in which kind fortune allowed me to take part.

Finally, I turned amid my press clippings to the reviews of some of the war books which recorded those years and were published between thirty and forty years ago. They bring back the names of some still-living authors whose work seems likely to endure, such as Edmund Blunden and Robert Graves. Among them I find an anniversary article in the London *Times* by no less a personality than its former editor, Sir William Haley.

Writing as Oliver Edwards, the pseudonym that he adopted for the literary articles that he contributed to the columns of his paper, he included an assessment of the books which were, in his view, the most memorable to come out of the First World War. In this article he described *Testament of Youth*, published by Victor Gollancz in London in August, 1933, and by the Macmillan companies of New York and Toronto shortly afterwards, as 'the war book of the Women of England'.

This was not, perhaps, quite the tribute that it might have appeared, for relatively few women played an active part in the First World War. They were, on the whole, merely aides operating behind the various fronts. Such roles as they did fulfill were modest, subsidiary, and insignificant. War was a man's business. In 1914 the women who volunteered to serve as nurses with the Scottish Women's Hospitals in areas where qualified women of any description were extremely scarce were told by the Establishment to 'go home and keep quiet'. This was, it seemed, in masculine opinion the only useful thing that women could do.

Even after the war was over, women of relevant age were not regarded as having had any real contact with its realities. Some years after my own direct experience had ended, I came to know a cultured and critical young man named Roy Randall who wrote for several highbrow weeklies. His literary ambitions were unlimited, and he liked to discuss them with me. Occasionally, out of politeness, he referred to the modest freelance journalism by which I was struggling to find a foothold in the writing world.

One day, much to my embarrassment, he asked me what work I hoped to undertake in the near future. I had then published two short novels and three unimportant little volumes of nonfiction and was living largely on the meagre proceeds of my freelance articles and book reviews. After three or four years of intimidated and spasmodic endeavour, I was also trying to draft the outline of *Testament of Youth* and did not want to disclose the ambitious character of this effort, which I knew that my companion would regard as extremely presumptuous. So when Roy pressed me for an answer, I replied vaguely that I was trying to do 'a kind of autobiography'.

His contemptuous reply was even more devastating than I had foreseen:

'An autobiography! But I shouldn't have thought that anything in *your* life was worth recording!'

This shattering judgment, though it shook my equilibrium, did not put me off my project. At that time I had served for four gruelling years in London, France, and the Mediterranean and had seen my nearest and dearest contemporaries – lover, brother, and two much-loved friends – hounded to death in the holocaust of a male generation. But knowing that my appearance still suggested that of a half-fledged university student I did not protest but merely resolved with the more determination to record while light lasted the events that I remembered.

When I related this conversation at a dinner with my near contemporary Rebecca West and her husband, Henry Andrews, Henry seemed disposed to agree with the sceptical Roy, but Rebecca, echoing my private thoughts, turned on him and said: 'You mean she's not a field marshal? But it's the psychological kind of autobiography that succeeds nowadays, not the old dull kind.'

The idea of a war book had come with the publication of memoirs by some of the few male literary contemporaries who had survived the War. It was also provoked by sheer perversity. I knew well that no one expected a woman to understand anything about war, much less to try to record it. But it must have come into my mind soon after the first performance of R.C. Sherriff's *Journey's End* – that famous swallow that was to make a summer – which I saw with Winifred Holtby, the author of *South Riding*, when we realized that an electric atmosphere of reminiscent emotion had replaced the mere *succès d'estime* which we had both expected.

Soon after seeing the play and reading the too poignant published memoirs, I began to ask myself: 'Why should these young men have the war to themselves? Didn't women have their war as well? They weren't all, as these men make them out to be, only suffering wives and mothers, or callous parasites, or mercenary prostitutes. Does no one remember the women who began their war service with such high ideals or how grimly they carried on when that flaming faith had crumbled into the grey ashes of disillusion? Who will write the epic of the women who went to the war, and came back leaving the bones of their men in the trampled fields of France and amid the grey rocks of the Asiago Plateau?'

Could I, who had done nothing important yet, carry through such a massive undertaking? With scientific precision, I studied the memoirs of Blunden, Sassoon, and Graves. Surely, I thought, my story is as interesting as theirs. Besides, I see things other than they have seen, and some of the things they perceived, I see differently.

The kind of memoir that could be written only by a prime minister or an ambassador, I believed with Rebecca West, was ceasing to have much appeal. A new type of autobiography was coming into fashion, which would represent the ordinary people of the world upon whom wars were imposed. I wanted to make my own story as truthful as history but as readable as fiction, and in it I intended to speak, not for those in high places, but for my own generation of obscure young women.

Inspired by blind faith and the urgent need for reconciliation with the past, I began to collect and reread letters and memoirs and to try to assess the significance of my own adventures which Roy Randall had thought so trivial. I soon realized how typical they were – not so much in terms of women's experience, as of that of an entire generation. The details of our lives had naturally differed; there was clearly a great contrast at that date between the stories of men and women. But we all had experienced the tremendous revolution – one of the greatest in history – which carried the nineteenth century into the twentieth. It became my intention to attempt to estimate the apocalyptic quality of these changes which transformed forever the world into which my contemporaries and I were born.

Vera with Edith and Arthur Brittain, *circa* 1911

A woman could perceive the picture as dearly as a man – perhaps more clearly, owing to the inevitably greater detachment which a woman's wartime insignificance gave her. Gradually now I began to perceive my 'war book' as a vehicle for the picture of a vast age of transition, slowly becoming evident through the illuminating details which changed as each disastrous, tragic, and dramatic epoch merged into another.

Midway between the beginning and end of the war I had written to my brother in the trenches about the quality of our age. He was then on the Italian Front and, though only twenty-one, was the kind of correspondent who understands everything. Such individuals are so rare that I have missed him all my life and still wish that I could refer to him some of the problems that I now have to face.

About the summer of 1917 I wrote to him: 'I think that "Before" and "After" this war will make the same kind of division in human history as "BC" and "AD"' At the time this seemed an extravagant and even absurd assessment, but after half a century it does not seem to me that I was so far wrong in my estimate of that tremendous perspective.

The quality of the two titanic revolutions was, of course, quite different. The transition from the pagan to the Christian world meant a vast spiritual change affecting all human lives from the first century onward; it challenged existing values irrespective of whether those challenged understood the issues involved.

The changes created by the events of 1914 and the years immediately afterward were social and political, but they, too, were apocalyptic and fundamental. Mankind was never the same again after 1914, any more than it was ever the same again after the Crucifixion. Only those who recall, however dimly, the vanishing sunset splendour of the final Victorian years can estimate in their personal histories the quality of the transformation which the events of 1914 created for the much battered human race.

The normal experience of mortal life has been one of war and catastrophe. This was a fact very difficult to realize by the young of my generation. In spite of the tragedies and errors of the South African War – which are only now fully reaching realization in the spiritual bankruptcy of apartheid – our earliest memories, especially if we came from the ever-growing middle classes, are of prosperity and security. These ultimately proved as ephemeral as most varieties of good fortune, giving rise to such cynical obiter dicta as 'Life is the predicament that precedes death.' But at the time they seemed permanent – a fact that explains the contrast between the poets of the two war generations. The work of Sassoon and his near contemporaries was one long cry of protest precisely because they were the products of an exceptionally fortunate social era. When their Second War successors reached adulthood, the world had reverted to the normal human experience of frustration and disappointment, and the horrors of war casualties offered a less emphatic contrast with preceding events.

In the verses entitled 'The War Generation: Ave', with which I opened Chapter 1 of *Testament of Youth*, I endeavoured to put into words the innocent contentment of late Victorian childhood, especially among those born far from the influence of formative political events.

In cities and in hamlets we were born,
And little towns behind the van of time;
A closing era mocked our guileless dawn
With jingles of a military rhyme.
But in that song we heard no warning chime,
Nor visualized in hours benign and sweet
The threatening woe that our adventurous feet
Would starkly meet.

Thus we began, amid the echoes blown
Across our childhood from an earlier war,
Too dim, too soon forgotten, to dethrone
Those dreams of happiness we thought secure;
While, imminent and fierce outside the door,
Watching a generation grow to flower,
The late that held our youth within its power
Waited its hour.

The belief that individuals were entitled to expect peace and hap-
piness as their normal fate took so long to die that remnants of it still
came to life even when the First War had been over for years. In
1939, when I took my son, then a boy of twelve, to his preparatory
school for his first term, I happened to make a conventional com-
ment to his headmaster about the misfortune for a child of having to
begin his schooldays in a year when the unhappy history of my own
generation was about to repeat itself in a series of dire events. The
headmaster, a grave Quaker, mildly reprimanded me for the lack
of historical perspective of which I seemed to him to be guilty.

'Think what it must have meant to start your education at the beginning of the Thirty Years' War!'

But for all its problems which affected our children as those of the First War did not, I have never been able to feel that September 3rd, 1939, presented a comparable cataclysm to that of August 4th, 1914. The second date had been long foreseen, and though it heralded more and worse disasters which were to come closer to the comfortable British people than the cross-Channel terrors of the First World War, it lacked the same quality of shock. It was that sense of shock which, as it came into perspective, eclipsed all the other and more recent memories.

The entry from Vera's diary for August 1914, describing
the outbreak of war

What does that date, August 4th, 1914, immediately bring back to me? Not, certainly, the recollection of gunrunning in Ulster which so oddly preceded much greater anxieties, or yet the assassination of the Archduke Franz Ferdinand, though it was soon associated with macabre rumours that blood had been seen on the sun and moon. The immediate memories are purely personal and do not concern the statistics of world transformation, though I was to give so much attention to them later. The huge figures of the war casualties and the cost of war expenditure vanish in a phantasmagoria of human scenes and sounds. I think, instead, of names, places, and individuals and hear, above all, the echo of a boy's laughing voice on a school playing field in that golden summer.

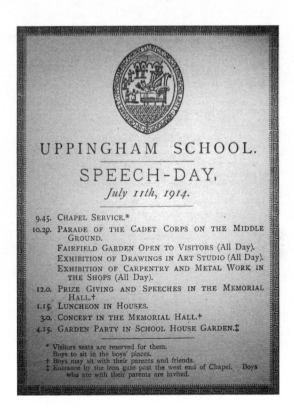

UPPINGHAM SCHOOL.

SPEECH-DAY,

July 11th, 1914.

9.45. CHAPEL SERVICE.*

10.20. PARADE OF THE CADET CORPS ON THE MIDDLE
GROUND.
FAIRFIELD GARDEN OPEN TO VISITORS (All Day).
EXHIBITION OF DRAWINGS IN ART STUDIO (All Day).
EXHIBITION OF CARPENTRY AND METAL WORK IN
THE SHOPS (All Day).

12.0. PRIZE GIVING AND SPEECHES IN THE MEMORIAL
HALL.†

1.15. LUNCHEON IN HOUSES.

3.0. CONCERT IN THE MEMORIAL HALL.†

4.15. GARDEN PARTY IN SCHOOL HOUSE GARDEN.‡

* Visitors seats are reserved for them.
Boys to sit in the boys' places.
† Boys may sit with their parents and friends.
‡ Entrance by the iron gate past the west end of Chapel. Boys
who are with their parents are invited.

And gradually the voice becomes one of many; the sound of
the Uppingham School choir marching up the chapel for
the Speech Day service in July 1914, and singing the
Commemoration hymn:

> O Merciful and Holy
> Who once by ways unknown
> In simple hearts and lowly

Dost build Thy loftiest throne,
As Thou of old wast near us
To bless our Founder's care,
Bow down Thine ear and hear us
In this, Thy house of prayer.

There was a thrilling, a poignant quality in those boys' voices, as though they were singing their own requiem – as indeed many of them were. Among these were my brother, Edward, and his best friend, the prizewinning Roland Leighton, who had hoped to marry me and become a *Times* leader writer, but instead found a lowly grave amid the white crosses which marked the Somme even before the great battles of 1916 were fought. But when the personal memories are, with difficulty, banished, it is the suddenness and shock of the whole event which remains with me longest.

Many years before the Great War, George Eliot, though she lived in one of history's calmest centuries, had prophetically visualized the situation of the war generation in her novel *Daniel Deronda*:

There comes a terrible moment to many souls when the great movements of the world, the larger destinies of mankind, which have lain aloof in newspapers and other neglected reading, enter like an earthquake into their own lives – when the slow urgency of growing generations turns into the tread of an invading army or the dire clash of civil war. Then it is that the submission of the soul to the Highest is tested and . . . life looks out from the scene of human struggle with the awful face of duty.

That 'awful face of duty' sent the generation which had known no major war since their grandparents had fought in the Crimea into the interminable miles of trenches which stretched from the Ardennes to the North Sea or took them in the ships, great and small, which when they were sunk carried hundreds of young men – many of them midshipmen barely in their teens – into a cold anonymous grave without hope of rescue or the least understanding of the issue for which they had sacrificed their lives. They belonged to a sheltered human vintage for which occasional disasters, such as the sinking of the *Titanic* in 1912, were isolated reminders that tragedy existed. But no one, before 1914, expected it to come nearer, for smooth events had established the conviction that human happiness was normal and disaster exceptional; those to whom it happened were thought to be particularly unlucky.

To us, with our cheerful confidence in the benignity of fate, war was something remote, unimaginable, its monstrous destructions and distresses safely shut up, like the Black Death and the Great Fire, between the covers of history books. In spite of the efforts of a few percipient teachers who taught a generation of schoolchildren unaccustomed to read the newspapers to take an interest in at least the headlines, 'current events' had remained unimportant just because they were national; they represented 'subjects' that were habitually taught in classrooms but would never, conceivably, have to be lived.

What really mattered were not these public issues, but the absorbing incidents of our private lives – our careers, ambitions, friendships, and love affairs. And now, with the suddenness that

George Eliot had described, the one had impinged on the other, and public issues and private lives had become bewilderingly inseparable. The significance of these events did not become clear until those who had suffered them began to write about them – which meant that they had to think about them. In some cases, as in my own, the thinking process lasted for years before it was decanted into words. And part of the process showed that *anyone* whom those years concerned was entitled to assess them – young or old, men or women. War was a human event, not a happening which affected one age or sex rather than another.

Yet if the whole comfortable generation had felt sheltered and secure, its women seemed to be especially cut off from reality. Their subservience was not a matter for discussion except by a handful of wild fanatics who had begun to make extravagant claims to equality and opportunity. The inferiority of women was accepted as part of the natural order of creation. The suffragettes, to the amusement of the unthinking public, began to make their vehement demands, less than a decade before the world changed forever.

As I was to realize many years later when, at long last, the war insisted on being put into words, the very detachment of women from the most direct forms of active service impressed on me once and for all the domination by war between 1914 and 1919 of even the most trivial aspects of everyday life. The war could not be escaped even by the most skillfully devised plays, books, and concerts. It permeated the arts; in my first year at Oxford the Bath Choir, which I had joined, gave a moving performance of the Verdi *Requiem* which haunts me to this day, and I still remember listening at Southwark Cathedral in July 1916 to the Brahms *Requiem* which so poignantly coincided with the first day of the tremendous Somme battle. Even today the First War atmosphere is immediately brought back to me by the plaintive notes of Cowper's hymn 'God moves in a mysterious way', so often sung at church services by congregations growing ever more anxious to be consoled and reassured.

The wearing anxiety of waiting for letters probably made all noncombatants feel more distracted than anything else in that sustained nightmare. Even when the letters came, they were at least four days old; the writers after sending them would have had time to die many times. This particular form of painful suspense, which had to be ignored on duty with as much resolution as the individual could muster, began for me when Roland Leighton went to the Front as a boy barely twenty in March 1915 and ended for me only in June 1918, when my brother's death after that of Roland and our two dearest friends left me with no one else for whom to feel anxiety.

During the periods of waiting, especially when the newspapers, with inevitable vagueness, reported the imminence of a 'great push', ordinary household sounds became a torment. The striking of a clock, marking off each hour of dread, broke into the immobility of tension with the shattering effect of a thunderclap. Every ring at the bell suggested a telegram, the only method of conveying urgent news before the days of radio and television; every telephone call implied a long-distance message giving bad news.

The extent of this torment naturally varied with both the quality of individual imagination and the measure of personal involvement. Probably I should never have been the only woman to contribute to this symposium had not my own involvement been so deep and so continuous. Even today, after fifty years, it still seems to me almost incredible that during those four years there actually were women who had no friends or relatives in the trenches or on the perilous seas, who were not perpetually waiting for messages of disaster. It is not surprising that many women developed an anxiety neurosis which lasted until the end of their lives.

To this constant dread was added, as the end of the fighting moved ever onward into an incalculable future, a new fear that the war would come between the men at the front and the women who loved them. Between 1914 and 1919 the war always did, putting a barrier of indescribable experience between the two sexes, thrusting horror deeper and deeper inward, linking the dread of spiritual death to the apprehension of physical disaster. When one of two dear friends was blinded at Arras in 1917 and sent to England to die in a London military hospital, I went to his funeral in Sussex, where his family lived. More bitter even than the sorrow of his death was my acute consciousness of England's uncomprehending remoteness from the tragic, profound freemasonry which united the men and, very rarely, the women who accepted death together overseas.

The women who served or only waited in the Second World War, though they experienced fresh horrors and many other dangers, such as the V-1s and V-2s with their incalculable descents on undefended targets, were at least spared this fear of estrangement due to ignorance, for in this second onslaught of fate men and women alike shared the perils that threatened both sexes. In some countries, such as Germany, which endured the terror of saturation raids by British and American bombers, women faced greater risks than their men, who had at least better protection in the forces than in the barely defended small towns and villages in or near the major target areas, such as Kiel and Hamburg, and the vulnerable closely packed cities of the Ruhr.

I recall reading in a German newspaper quoted in England about 1944 of the distress experienced by a group of servicemen traveling on leave from the Russian Front to their homes in Hamburg, then virtually extinguished by the merciless raids on civilian areas of 1942–4. Standing in the corridor of their train, these soldiers, who had been out of Germany for two or three years, were rendered almost speechless by seeing the ruins of their homes and 'bowing before the sacrifice'.

This meant that the experiences of the women of the First World War were, in fact, unique and probably could not now be duplicated by any woman in any war – irrespective of the certainty that no woman and no man would be likely to survive a major conflict at all. In such a conflict, as Shakespeare wrote in *The Tempest*:

> The cloud-capp'd towers, the gorgeous palaces,
> The solemn temples, the great globe itself,
> Yea, all which it inherit, shall dissolve;
> And, like this insubstantial pageant faded,
> Leave not a rack behind.

Assuming, meanwhile, that the menaced human race can count on a few more years of life on its insecure planet, the two wars, surprisingly, went far to solve the problems involved by women's social and political status, a matter with which I have always been deeply concerned. The myth of female inferiority has always been rooted in the contention that men die for their country but women do not. Now neither sex, except in very primitive societies, can do this with any expectation that their efforts will be effective against the colossal amoralities of dominant science. If any of us is to have a future on this earth, it must depend on man's ability to reconquer his power over the machine, which he yielded in the First World War.

When I finally went down in 1921 from the Oxford that, in spite of parental scepticism, I had first tried to enter in 1914 (winning an exhibition to everybody's astonishment, including my own), I was just in time to take part in the struggle for degrees for women, which Oxford granted twenty-seven years before Cambridge.

The war was often said to be responsible for the immediate postwar feminist reforms in Britain, and indeed it helped, in the sense that it did give women the opportunity to show that they could do what they had long claimed. These results would not, however, have achieved their purpose without the preliminary years of feminist spadework, ending in the spectacular protests of the suffragettes, who put the women's cause on the map.

But in a much deeper sense the two wars made the sexes equal, not merely because women proved that they could do the work of men (as they did), but because they could, and did, die the deaths of men. Thus, they shared the 'supreme sacrifice', which made them equals in death as in life.

The implications of this immense social fact have still to be worked out in this second half of the twentieth century, which has sent so many women into key positions in public life and given them an equal share of such human experience as any of us alive today can hope to achieve.

Vera in 1942

NOTES

ABBREVIATIONS

Diary   *Chronicle of Youth. Vera Brittain's War Diary 1913–1917*, edited by Alan Bishop with Terry Smart. London: Gollancz, 1981.

Letters   *Letters from a Lost Generation. First World War Letters of Vera Brittain and Four Friends*, edited by Alan Bishop and Mark Bostridge. London: Little, Brown, 1998.

Life   Paul Berry and Mark Bostridge, *Vera Brittain: A Life*. London: Chatto & Windus, 1995.

McM   Vera Brittain Archive, McMaster University, Hamilton, Ontario.

PWA   Vera Brittain, *Poems of the War and After*. London: Victor Gollancz, 1934.

TY   Vera Brittain, *Testament of Youth*. [London: Victor Gollancz 1933].Virago new edition, with an introduction by Mark Bostridge, 2004.

VB   Vera Brittain

VVAD   Vera Brittain, *Verses of a V.A.D.*, London: Erskine Macdonald, 1918.

INTRODUCTION

p. xiii **'The noble deeds'**: VB, 'A Tribute to King Edward VII. Written at the time of his death'. *St Monica's School Notes, 1910–1911*. McM.

p. xiii **one of her final school essays**: Essay in 'Juvenilia'. McM.

p. xvi **'real Active Service conditions'**: VB to Edith and Arthur Brittain, 5 August 1917. McM.

p. xvi **'history's greatest disaster'**: *TY*, 3.

p. xvii **'has not only stimulated'**: *Mr Punch's History of the Great War* (London: Cassell, 1919), 247. Of the 2225 British men and women identified as publishing poems about the war between 1914 and 1918, it has been estimated that at least 532 of them were women. See Catherine Reilly, *English Poetry of the First World War: A Bibliography* (London, 1978).

p. xvii **'and the only kind'**: *TY*, 115. VB did complete the draft of a novel called 'The Pawn of Fate' in the closing months of the War. It was set in a French military hospital at 'Echy', which was clearly based on the 24 General at Etaples. See *Life*, 236–7.

p. xvii **'poetry counteracts'**: *TY*, 397.

p. xvii **'an irredeemable loneliness'**: Paul Fussell, *The Great War and Modern Memory* (Oxford: Oxford University Press), 297.

p. xvii . . . **to Edward that Vera often turned**: E.g., 'About the poems – The Last Post is best . . . the German Ward is a good idea and a good picture . . .' Edward Brittain to VB, 24 October 1917. McM.

p. xvii **'considerateness and tender sympathy . . . author's'**: *VVAD*, 10–11.

p. xviii **'the one perfect'**: *TY*, 72.

p. xviii **'He seems'**: *Diary*, 81.

p. xix **'In this time'**: *Diary*, 135.

p. xx **'Villanelle'**: Printed in *TY*, 114.

p. xx **'I handed it back to him'**: *Diary*, 250.

p. xx **'so sad'**: *Diary*, 195.

p. xx **'seemed to stir'**: *Diary*, 207.

p. xxi **'the fleshless, blackened bones'**: Roland Leighton to VB, 11 September 1915. *Letters*, 165.

p. xxii **'always been so much'**: VB to Edith Brittain, 20 April 1917. *Letters*, 337.

p. xxiii **'a very close'**: VB to Edward Brittain, 6 May 1917. *Letters*, 350.

p. xxiii **'My dear dear Geoffrey'**: *Diary*, 340–1.

p. xxiii **'I am so glad'**: VB to Edith Brittain, 25 September 1917. McM.

p. xxiii **'please send'**: VB to Edith Brittain, 24 October 1917. McM.

p. xxiii **'an experimental publisher'**: VB, *On Becoming a Writer* (London: Hutchinson, 1947), 177.

p. xxiv **'Young soldiers'**: Dominic Hibberd and John Onions, *The Winter of the World. Poems of the First World War* (London: Constable, 2007), xxii. Galloway Kyle was exposed in a court case in 1922. See Dominic

Hibberd, *Owen the Poet* (London: Macmillan, 1986), 63.

p. xxiv **'free of all costs'**: 'Memorandum of Agreement' between VB and Erskine Macdonald Ltd, 8 June 1918. McM.

p. xxiv **'Very glad'**: Edward Brittain to VB, 10 February 1918. *Letters*, 389.

p. xxiv **'I have written'**: VB to Edith Brittain, 3 March 1918. McM.

p. xxiv **'would do something'**: VB to Edith Brittain, 10 March 1918. McM.

p. xxiv **'What is Erskine Macdonald'**: Edward Brittain to VB, 24 May 1918. McM.

p. xxv **'well-finished'**: *Times Literary Supplement*, 19 September 1918.

p. xxv **The *Athenaeum***: *Athenaeum*, January 1919.

p. xxv **'Their want of elaboration'**: *Aberdeen Free Press*, 23 October 1918.

p. xxv **'Excellent prose'**: *Yorkshire Observer*, 7 January 1919.

p. xxv **'while watching'**: VB to Edith Brittain, 15 September 1917. McM.

p. xxv **'One talks'**: VB to Edith Brittain, 10 March 1918. McM.

p. xxvi **Critics of women's poetry**: See in particular Janet Montefiore, '"Shining Pins and Wailing Shells": Women Poets and the Great War' in *Women and World War 1: The Written Response*, edited by Dorothy Goldman (London: Macmillan, 1993). Nosheen Khan, *Women's Poetry of the First World War* (Brighton: Harvester, 1988) places a wide range of women poets from 1914 to 1918 in their contemporary context.

p. xxvi **Catherine Reilly's pioneering anthology**: *Scars Upon My Heart: Women's Poetry and Verse of the First World War*, edited by Catherine Reilly (London: Virago, 1981).

p. xxvii **'as I could never'**: *TY*, 396.

p. xxvii **'It begins'**: Simon Featherstone, 'Mina Loy and E.J. Scovell: Defining Women's War Poetry' in *The Oxford Handbook of British and Irish War Poetry*, edited by Tim Kendall (Oxford: Oxford University Press, 2007), 446.

p. xxviii ***Oxford Poetry***: VB was co-editor, with C.H.B. Kitchen and Alan Porter, of the volume for 1920.

p. xxviii ***Poems of the War and After***: This also republished all the poems from *Verses of a V.A.D.* VB wrote in the foreword that the book was published 'chiefly for those readers of *Testament of Youth* who have asked me where they can obtain my long-defunct little volume *Verses* *of a VAD*, which went out of print soon after publication in the usual manner of experimental verses by immature writers'.

p. xxviii **'They're with me always'**: VB to Winifred Holtby, 11 November 1921. Winifred Holtby Archive, Hull Central Library.

p. xxviii **This spiritualist revival**: The subjects of 'Spiritualism and the Lost Generation', and of Sir Oliver Lodge's *Raymond*, are discussed by Jay Winter in *Sites of Memory, Sites of Mourning. The Great War in European Cultural History* (Cambridge: Cambridge University Press, 1995), 54–77.

p. xxix **Nina Ruffer**: daughter of Sir Armand Ruffer, the medical chief of the British Red Cross Society in Egypt, who had been drowned in 1917 when the ship on which he was travelling was torpedoed.

p. xxix **'Miss Ruffer'**: VB to Edith Brittain, 22 June 1919. McM. VB does not allude to her experience of spiritualism in TY.

p. xxx **'brutal, poignant'**: VB to Elizabeth Nicholas, 16 October 1961. Quoted in *Life*, 236.

p. xxxi **'war is a glorious thing'**: See below, page 175.

p. xxxii **'Well Malta'**: VB to Edith Brittain, 5 August 1917. *Letters*, 368–9.

p. xxxii **like a large town**: See Douglas Gill and Julian Putkowski, *Le Camp Britannique d'Etaples* (Etaples: Musée Quentovic, 1998) for an account of the encampment. Today, the Commonwealth cemetery, designed by Lutyens with its extraordinary pylons and arched cenotaphs flanked by stone flags, covers part of the area of the base camp. The site of the 24 General is to be found among a small group of houses in the Avenue du Blanc Pavé.

p. xxxii **'Disturbance in Reinforcement Camp'**: National Archives WO 95/4085. VB's account of the mutiny at Etaples in *Testament of Youth*, inaccurate as it was, was only the second to appear in print. The first, by Lady Angela Forbes, who had run a canteen at the base, was published in 1924.

p. xxxiii **'more or less dying'**: VB to Edith Brittain, 5 August 1917. *Letters*, 368.

p. xxxiii **this discrepancy**: It was first noted by Douglas Gill in 'No Compromise with Truth. Vera Brittain in 1917', *Krieg und Literatur*, V, 1999. The records of the 24 General, kept by Colonel Penton (National

Archives WO 95/4085) show that a total of thirty German officers and men died at the 24 General in the period 4–31 August 1917, and only four German patients in the period 1–15 September 1917: rates of mortality, respectively, of 3 per cent and less than 2 per cent.

p. xxxiii **she initially exaggerated**: VB's report of large numbers of German prisoners dying belongs to a letter written soon after her arrival, and was not repeated subsequently by her in later correspondence.

p. xxxiv **BBC Television's landmark documentary**: See Dan Todman, *The Great War. Myth and Memory* (London: Continuum, 2006), 182.

p. xxxiv *Yesterday's Witness*: For an account of the interview, see *Life*, 521.

p. xxxv **the only woman**: The writer Storm Jameson was asked to contribute, but refused owing to pressure of work. VB was included at the suggestion of Sir Karl Popper.

p. xxxv 'An incisive': George Panichas to VB, 15 August 1967. McM.

p. xxxv 'but the absorbing': See below, page 201.

PART ONE: POETRY

The place of first publication is given in italics. All of the poems published in *Verses of a V.A.D.* (1918) are included in *Poems of the War and After* (1934). The dating of individual poems is taken from the notebooks (D98, D105, D106, and D107) in the Vera Brittain Archive at McMaster University, Hamilton, Ontario.

AUGUST 1914
VVAD
Written at Somerville College, Oxford, towards the end of 1914, during VB's first term as an undergraduate, and originally called 'By Reason of His Mercy'.

... **redemption comes through pain**: An echo of Olive Schreiner's novel, *The Story of an African Farm* (1883), given by Roland Leighton to VB in April 1914, the book quickly became VB's personal bible and a leitmotiv of her ultimately tragic wartime relationship with Roland. Schreiner had written that 'The lifting up of the hands brings no salvation; redemption is from within, and neither from God nor man: it is wrought out by the soul itself, with suffering and through time.'

ST PANCRAS STATION, AUGUST 1915
VVAD
On 20 August 1915 Roland Leighton, on leave from France, met VB at St Pancras Station. They became unofficially engaged 'for three years or the duration of the War'. After spending a night with the Brittains and a few days at Lowestoft with his family, Roland saw Vera off from St Pancras on 23 August. She was reporting for duty at the Devonshire Hospital in Buxton, where she was starting work as a probationary VAD. Roland returned to billets with the 7th Worcesters on 26 August.

TO A FALLEN IDOL
VVAD
The poem may refer to Maurice Ellinger, VB and Edward Brittain's friend from Buxton who, like Edward, was a pupil at Uppingham School. In June 1913 Maurice Ellinger had been expelled from Uppingham for 'immorality'. In 1915, he made a failed attempt at suicide.

TO MONSEIGNEUR
VVAD
Addressed to Roland Leighton and written in November 1915 while VB was a VAD at the 1st London General Hospital, in Cormont Road, Camberwell. 'Monseigneur' was Roland's nickname at Uppingham School where he had been a pupil from 1909 to 1914.

Roland of Roncesvalles: The leader of a band of brave warriors surrounding Charlemagne, who perished at Roncesvalles in northern Spain in 778. Roland's legend found its most famous expression in twelfth-century France, in the *Chanson de Roland*.

THE ONLY SON
VVAD
The 'Only Son' was VB's younger brother Edward.

PERHAPS—
VVAD
On the night of 22 December 1915 Roland Leighton was mortally wounded by German sniper fire while inspecting the barbed wire in front of a trench at Hébuterne.

He died at eleven o'clock the following evening, after an operation at the casualty clearing station at Louvencourt to remove a bullet from his spine.

A draft of 'Perhaps—' was written at the 1st London General in February 1916. The poem was completed in August of that year.

A MILITARY HOSPITAL
VVAD
Written at the 1st London General, Camberwell, in March 1916.

LOOKING WESTWARD
VVAD
August 1916

THEN AND NOW
VVAD
'πάντα ῥεῖ καὶ οὐδένα μένι': This is the most famous aphorism of the pre-Socratic philosopher Heraclitus. It means 'everything flows and nothing stands still'.

MAY MORNING
Oxford Magazine, 5 May 1916 ('May Morning at Oxford'); *VVAD*. Originally subtitled 'At Oxford – and After'.
VB is remembering her first May Morning at Oxford, in 1915. She had described it in a letter to Roland in France (*Letters*, 95): 'I was up at 3.45 this morning for the famous May Morning ceremony . . . as the clock struck four

all the people turned towards the tower & became absolutely silent. Then immediately after, as the sun was rising, the choristers on the top of Magdalen tower sang the May Morning Latin hymn, turning towards the sun . . . I could quite easily have wept at the beauty & pain of it. I couldn't help thinking how different everything is from what we pictured it would be, & how you meant to be here, & how you would have loved it if you had been . . .'

THE TWO TRAVELLERS
VVAD
July 1916
This poem later provided the inspiration for the title of Winifred Holtby's second novel, *The Crowded Street* (1924), where it appears as the novel's epigraph.

THE SISTERS BURIED AT LEMNOS
Oxford Magazine, 11 May 1917; VVAD.
October 1916
Written by VB while on board the hospital ship *Britannic* in September–October 1916, when she was one of a party of VADs sailing to Malta to nurse. The sisters buried at Lemnos were Canadians, who had nursed at the camp there.

'FIDELIS AD EXTREMUM': faithful to the extreme.

IN MEMORIAM: G.R.Y.T.
VVAD
1 May 1917
VB and Geoffrey (Robert Youngman) Thurlow had become close friends in the period following Roland Leighton's death. On 30 April 1917, while nursing in Malta, VB learned of Geoffrey's death in action at Monchy-le-Preux, in an attack on the Scarpe on 23 April.

A PARTING WORD
VVAD
26 May 1917

Originally entitled 'To one more fortunate than I', this poem was addressed to Stella Sharp, VB's schoolfriend from St Monica's, who served with her as a VAD in London and Malta. VB resented the fact that Stella, in enjoying the society of naval and medical officers on Malta, had chosen to neglect her old friend.

THE TROOP TRAIN
VVAD
27 May 1917
Written as VB made her return journey from Malta to England by rail through France. In the final entry of her wartime diary for that day, VB wrote: 'Left Amiens at last, went through Abbeville & Etaples. Etaples seemed one vast & very dusty camp; we were much cheered by the Tommies in a troop train that we passed, & cheered & waved to by the soldiers in the camps along both sides of the railway. Made me very glad I had elected to be a nurse & remain one, instead of doing something else.' (*Diary*, 341).

SIC TRANSIT—
VVAD
9 June 1917
On 9 April Victor Richardson, Roland and Edward's schoolfriend from Uppingham, had been injured in an attack on a heavily defended German entrenchment three miles north of Arras. Victor lost his left eye and the sight of his right was also threatened. VB returned from Malta on 28 May, intending to devote her life to the service of Victor in memory of Roland. But on 8 June there was a serious deterioration in Victor's condition and he died early the following morning.

TO THEM
VVAD
24 June 1917
Written on the day of Edward Brittain's return to his battalion in France. Edward had enjoyed a long period of convalescent leave, following the action on the first day of the Battle of the Somme, in July 1916, in which he was wounded.

OXFORD REVISITED
VVAD
27 June 1917

THE GERMAN WARD
VVAD
September 1917
On 4 August 1917, the third anniversary of the outbreak of war, VB
arrived at the 24 General, Etaples, and was assigned to Ward 29, where
for five weeks she nursed German prisoners of war. 'You will be surprised
to hear that at present I am nursing German prisoners,' she wrote to her
mother on 5 August. 'My ward is entirely reserved for the most acute
German surgical cases; we have no cases but the very worst (26 beds) &
a theatre is attached to the ward . . . The majority are more or less dying;
never, even at the First London General during the Somme push, have I
seen such dreadful wounds . . . It gives one a chance to live up to our
Motto "Inter Arma Caritas", but anyhow one can hardly feel bitter
towards dying men. It is incongruous, though, to think of Edward in one
part of France trying to kill the same people whom in another part of
France I am trying to save . . .' (*Letters*, 368).

'**Inter Arma Caritas**': The Red Cross motto, 'Love amidst War'.

ROUNDEL
VVAD
February 1918

TO MY WARD-SISTER
VVAD
18 September 1918
Originally called 'In France – a Recollection'. Addressed to Sister Faith
Moulson (Hope Milroy in *TY*), a member of Queen Alexandra's Imperial
Military Nursing Service who was in charge of the German ward, and a
friend of VB's in France and after the war.

TO ANOTHER SISTER
VVAD
1918

In early December 1918 VB was moved to the acute medical ward of 24 General. Here she worked with a trained nurse known simply in TY as Mary, to whom this poem is dedicated.

WAR
VVAD
1918

On 21 March 1918 the German Commander Ludendorff launched a final desperate bid for victory against the Allied armies in the West. VB began this poem before the German Spring Offensive, but later used it to commemorate the event.

'VENGEANCE IS MINE'
VVAD
7 June 1918

At the end of April 1918, VB returned from France to 10 Oakwood Court in Kensington, having broken her VAD contract in response to her father's plea that she come home to care for her mother, who had suffered a breakdown and entered a nursing home.

A few weeks after her return, on the night of 19 May 1918, a German bombing raid on Etaples caused many casualties and much damage to the hospitals themselves, including the destruction of Ward 17 at the 24 General, where VB had nursed pneumonia cases on night duty. The raid was described in the following entry from the war diary of the Etaples Base Commandant (National Archives WO95/4027):

> 19/5/18. Area attacked by Enemy Aircraft. Casualties 1 Officer, 1 Nursing Sister. 167 OR [Other Ranks] killed; 27 Officers, 11 Nursing Sisters, 58 OR wounded; 18 OR missing. 1 Enemy Aircraft brought down. Crew of 3 captured. 1 Officer, 4 OR died in hospital.

There was a further raid on the night of 31 May/1 June.

While the British press was outraged by the bombing attacks, the authorities in France took a rather more circumspect view, as a report, dated August 1918 (National Archives WO32/5189), shows. The surviving German aircrew denied that they had been instructed to attack the hospitals and there was some controversy as to whether the red crosses used to identify the hospitals were visible from a bombing height of five thousand feet. In the end it was decided not to prosecute the German aircrew and it was recommended that, in future, hospitals should not be located near military camps, bridges, rail junctions or other legitimate targets.

The sentiments of the poem anticipate VB's campaign against the bombing of German cities during the Second World War (see *Life*, 436–42).

THE LAST POST
VVAD
1918

TO MY BROTHER
VVAD
11 June 1918
This poem, addressed to Edward Brittain, was written to commemorate his bravery on 1 July 1916, when he was wounded in the first wave of the British attack on the Somme, leading a company of the 11th Sherwood Foresters. VB inscribed it on the flyleaf of a copy of E. A. Osborn's popular anthology of war poetry, *The Muse in Arms* (1917), and sent it to Edward in Italy. But the poem arrived too late for him to read. He had been killed in action in the Austrian offensive on the Asiago Plateau, on 15 June 1918.

That cross you won: Edward had received the Military Cross 'for conspicuous gallantry and leadership during an attack' on 1 July 1916.

THAT WHICH REMAINETH
VVAD
16 July 1918

Only a Cross on a mountain side: Edward was buried in the British military cemetery at Granezza, four thousand feet up in the mountains. (See 'The Asiago Plateau' on pages 109–12 for a description of this cemetery).

THE ASPIRANT
VVAD
1918

REINSTATED
Previously unpublished. Manuscript in notebook D105 in VB Archive at McMaster University
September 1918
In September 1918 VB re-enlisted as a VAD but, as she had broken her contract to return from France, she discovered that she was ineligible for an immediate overseas posting. Instead she was forced to serve a further probationary period, first at London's St Thomas's Hospital and then at Queen Alexandra's Hospital on Millbank, where she nursed victims of the Spanish Flu epidemic.

A FAREWELL
PWA
1918
The image of a thrush 'gaily singing' is an allusion to Roland Leighton's final poem 'Hédauville', written in November 1915, a month before his death, in which he predicts that VB will meet 'Another Stranger'.

HOSPITAL SANCTUARY
PWA
September 1918

TO A VC
Oxford Magazine, 14 March 1919; *Oxford Poetry 1919*; PWA
September 1918
The recipient of the Victoria Cross referred to here was Lieutenant-

Colonel Charles Hudson (1892–1959), Edward's commanding officer whom VB pursued relentlessly with enquiries about Edward's death, convinced that Hudson was attempting to take the credit for some of act of gallantry performed by her brother in the battle in which he had been killed and Hudson badly wounded. In fact, Hudson was withholding information from VB about the prospect of a court martial, which Edward had faced in his last days because of alleged homosexual involvement with men in his company. Hudson only chose to reveal this to VB in 1934, following the publication of TY. (See *Life*, 127–35).

REQUIEM
PWA
November 1918
Written as the war came to an end, with the signing of the Armistice on 11 November 1918.

AFTER THREE YEARS
PWA
23 December 1918
Written to commemorate the third anniversary of Roland Leighton's death.

The April in my eyes ...: An echo of 'Nachlang', the poem Roland Leighton had written in April 1914 after he and VB and taken a long walk together, through Derbyshire's Goyt Valley and back to Buxton down Manchester Road. Roland had written of VB that 'there shone all April / In your eyes.'

FLOTSAM OF WAR
Previously unpublished. Manuscript in notebook D105 in VB Archive at McMaster University
1919

EPITAPH FOR EDWARD
PWA

May 1919
Written a month after VB's return to Somerville College, Oxford.

EPITAPH ON MY DAYS IN HOSPITAL
PWA
May 1919

TO ANY VICTIM OF CIRCUMSTANCES
PWA
1919

IN A SUMMERHOUSE
PWA
August 1919

THE END
PWA
1919

THE NEW STOICISM
PWA
1919

BOAR'S HILL, OCTOBER 1919
Oxford Poetry 1920; *PWA*

Boar's Hill: Situated just outside Oxford, from where there is a fine view
of the 'dreaming spires' of the city.

THE LAMENT OF THE DEMOBILISED
Oxford Chronicle, February 1920; *Oxford Poetry 1920*; *PWA*
17 January 1920
According to VB's Somerville contemporaries from 1919 to 1921, this
poem was addressed to the college's history tutor, the noted medievalist
Maude Clarke (1892–1935) who had pursued her academic career as an

undergraduate at Lady Margaret Hall, and then at Somerville, where she was appointed tutor in 1919, while VB was throwing 'four years into the melting pot' as a VAD. One of these contemporaries, Cicely Williams (1893–1992), later a distinguished paediatrician and nutritionist, maintained that VB confronted Maude Clarke and, in a bitter outburst, told her that but for the war she might have achieved academic distinction comparable to hers. This may well be so as an identical incident is included in VB's Oxford *roman-à-clef*, *The Dark Tide* (1923). (See *Life*, 148).

ANNIVERSARIES
Oxford Chronicle, February 1920; *PWA*
1920

THE SUPERFLUOUS WOMAN
PWA
25 July 1920
The idea of 'surplus women' – that the deaths of three-quarters of a million British men during the war meant that as many as a million women in Britain would be likely not to find husbands – became a popular scare story in the press during 1920. When the national census figures were published in 1921, the situation was confirmed as even worse than had been feared. In England and Wales there were 19,803,022 females and only 18,082,220 males, a difference of a million and three-quarters.

Surplus women also formed the subject matter of a poem by another woman poet of the war, Carola Oman (1897–1978), who, like VB, had served as a VAD in England and France. In 'The Lament of Many Women', published in her first book, *The Menin Road and Other Poems* (1919), Oman drew attention to those women labelled 'superfluous', who had lost husbands or lovers in the war.

THE UNSEEN UNDERGRADUATES
Oxford Chronicle, 1920; *PWA*
27 April 1919

WE SHALL COME NO MORE
PWA
1932
'The Island' is Malta, where VB served as a VAD in 1916–17.

THE WAR GENERATION: AVE
THE WAR GENERATION: VALE
PWA
March 1932
These poems were written for inclusion at the beginning and end of *TY*.

PART TWO: PROSE

24TH GENERAL HOSPITAL EXPEDITIONARY FORCE,
FRANCE
St Monica's School Notes, 1916–17
17 August 1917

Stella: Stella Sharp, VB's old schoolfriend who had served with her in Malta.

one forgets that they are the enemy: It is interesting to compare VB's attitude towards nursing German prisoners of war with that of another English nurse, Violetta Thurston, who nursed German soldiers in Belgium. Thurston comments on the irony of 'putting hundreds of cold compresses on German feet that they might be ready all the sooner to go out and kill our men'. After the soldiers leave her hospital, she feels 'a very joyful free sort of feeling at having got rid of the German patients'. Violetta Thurston, *Field Hospital and Flying Column: Being the Journal of an English Nursing Sister in Belgium* (Putnam, 1915), 158.

THE ASIAGO PLATEAU
Previously unpublished. Written *circa* 1923

King and Queen: George V and Queen Mary had gone to Italy on a state visit in the spring of 1923.

Caporetto: The Italian army had faced a humiliating rout at Caporetto in October 1917, during which their entire war effort had almost disintegrated. It was as a response to this that the 11th Sherwood Foresters, Edward Brittain's battalion, had been posted from France in November 1917 to join Allied reinforcements on the Italian Front, in the Alps above Vicenza.

the great battle ... on June 15th 1918: A decisive counter-offensive against the Austrian enemy, in which Edward Brittain had been killed.

'OUR BACKS TO THE WALL'. A MEMORY
Manchester Guardian, 3 February 1928

An Army Sister: Faith Moulson ('Hope Milroy' in *TY*). See note to 'To My Ward-Sister', above.

'THEIR NAME LIVETH'. FORGETTING WOMEN'S WAR-WORK
Manchester Guardian, 13 November 1929

Nurse Cavell: Edith Cavell (1865–1915). Cavell was arrested by the Germans and executed by firing squad on 12 October 1915, for helping British and French soldiers to escape from occupied Belgium. Her death was employed as a major propaganda weapon by the British government.

The Well of Loneliness: A lesbian novel by Radclyffe Hall (1880–1943), reviewed by VB on its publication in 1928. She found it 'a plea, passionate, yet admirably restrained and never offensive, for the extension of social toleration, compassion and recognition to the biologically abnormal woman', and was one of forty witnesses summoned by Hall's defence counsel when the book was prosecuted for obscenity in November 1928.

German war novels: The most famous of these was *Im Westen nichts Neues* by Erich Maria Remarque (1898–1970). Translated into English as *All Quiet on the Western Front*, and published in 1928, the novel sold a quarter of a million copies in its first year, and in 1930 was made into award-winning film by Lewis Milestone.

Journey's End: This trench drama by R.C. Sherriff (1896–1975) was a West End theatrical hit in 1929. VB saw the production with Winifred Holtby.

May Wedderburn Cannan: Arguably the finest woman poet of the First World War, Cannan (1893–1973) nursed as a VAD and in 1918 worked for MI5 in Paris. She was engaged to Bevis Quiller-Couch, who died of influenza in 1919 after serving in the army throughout the War. VB was to quote from Cannan's 'When the Vision Dies' in TY.

Death of a Hero: This semi-autobiographical novel by Richard Aldington (1892–1962) had appeared in 1929. It was widely viewed as a savage attack on wartime values.

All Else is Folly: Another anti-war book published in 1929. Its author was Peregrine Acland (1891–1963).

THE REAL VAD FROM FANCY BACK TO FACT
Manchester Guardian, 22 May 1930

The Forbidden Zone: Mary Borden (1886–1968) was a wealthy American living in England at the time of the outbreak of war in 1914. She used her own money to staff and equip a field hospital in France, where she served as a nurse until 1918. *The Forbidden Zone* is a remarkable series of stories and sketches based on her experiences, written with graphic realism. Some of them appeared, in 1917, in the *English Review*. The book was published in 1929.

It's a Great War!: A 1929 novel by the American writer Mary Lee (1891–1982), who had joined the Massachusetts General Hospital Unit on America's entry into the war in 1917, and had sailed to Europe to nurse. *It's a Great War!* won a competition for the best novel with the War as a background, but Lee had to share the prize when the prize committee objected to the fact that she was a woman.

Undertones of War: The war memoir by Edmund Blunden (1896–1974) was published in 1928.

WAAC: WAAC: *The Woman's Story of the War* was published anonymously in 1930.

Not So Quiet: *Not So Quiet . . . Stepdaughters of War* (1930) by Helen

Zenna Smith, the pseudonym of Evadne Price (1901–85), was a novel about women serving as ambulance drivers in France. It sold thousands of copies in Europe and the United States, and in France was awarded the Prix Séverigné as 'the novel most calculated to promote international peace'.

Brigadier-General Crozier: Frank Percy Crozier (1879–1937). Crozier had led the 9th Battalion Royal Irish Rifles in an assault on Thiepval on the first day of the Battle of the Somme, 1 July 1916. After the war he resigned his command of an auxiliary division of the Royal Ulster constabulary and tried to earn his living by writing. He became a pacifist and was an early supporter of the Peace Pledge Union, of which VB also became a sponsor.

French, Jellicoe, Foch and Mr Lloyd George: Sir John French (1852–1925), Commander-in-Chief, British Expeditionary Force in France, 1914–15; Admiral John Jellicoe (1859–1935), Commander-in-Chief, Grand Fleet, 1914, First Sea Lord, 1916; Ferdinand Foch (1851–1929), Allied Supreme Commander, 1918; David Lloyd George (1863–1945), Prime Minister, 1916–22.

A POPPY FOR HER COT. SOME ARMISTICE RECOLLECTIONS
Manchester Guardian, 11 November 1930

my two children: John Edward, born in December 1927, and Shirley Vivien, born in July 1930.

Mafeking and Ladysmith: The siege and relief of these two South African towns were celebrated events of the Boer War (1899–1902). VB's uncle Frank, her father's younger brother, was a farmer in South Africa when war broke out and was involved in the fighting for the defence of Ladysmith. He died of enteric, half an hour before the relief of the town in February 1900.

Kingsley's fabulous heroes: *The Heroes* by Charles Kingsley (1819–75) tells stories of Perseus, Theseus and the Argonauts for younger readers. It was a staple of the Edwardian schoolroom

RE-ENCOUNTER
Time and Tide, 31 December 1932

He'd played the violin so magnificently . . .: Like Richard, his fictional alter ego, Edward Brittain had shown promise as a musician, both as performer and composer.

WHILE WE REMEMBER. THE PURPOSE OF ARMISTICE DAY
Manchester Guardian, 11 November 1932

Wyndham Lewis: Writer and painter (1882–1957), who had been an official war artist during the First World War.

DIARY EXTRACT: SUMMER 1933
From VB's 'reflective record' of the thirties. The complete text of this extract may be found in VB, *Chronicle of Friendship. Vera Brittain's Diary of the Thirties 1932–1939*, edited by Alan Bishop. London: Gollancz, 1986.

Strachey's Menace of Fascism: A book by the former Labour MP, John Strachey (1901–63).

Norah Ashford: A senior VAD during VB's time at 24 General, Etaples, with whom VB had sometimes taken the sixteen-mile walk to Hardelot and back.

Pré Catalan: An old chateau that had been converted into a restaurant.

St J. Ervine: St John Ervine, a playwright, critic and novelist of Irish birth and irascible temperament (1883–1971), who was a great admirer of Winifred Holtby (she dedicated *The Astonishing Island* to him). For his letter, see *Life*, 263–4.

Stephen King-Hall: A writer and Independent politician (1893–1966).

Kiplingesque tradition: The writer Rudyard Kipling (1865–1936) had attacked British indifference towards the 'Tommy'.

Wickham Steed: A journalist and editor (1871–1956).

Sir John Hare: A well-known actor-manager (1844–1921).

Violet Scott-James: A journalist from Yorkshire (d. 1942) who was a close friend of Winifred Holtby.

1917 mutiny: Disturbances among Allied soldiers at the camp at Etaples, and in the town, had occurred between 9 and 12 September 1917 while VB was nursing at the 24 General.

Prince of Wales: Later Edward VIII (1894–1972), who abdicated in December 1936 and became the Duke of Windsor.

Lord Beaverbrook: The Canadian born newspaper magnate and Conservative politician (1879–1964).

Cry Havoc!: This anti-war book by Beverley Nichols (1898–1983), VB's Oxford contemporary in 1919–21, caused a furore on its publication in July 1933. Described by Nichols himself as a work of idealistic pacifism, it was labelled by one reviewer as 'not so much a book as a scream'.

1921, 1924, 1933 travels: VB had travelled in Europe with Winifred Holtby during the summers of these years. In 1924 they were accredited journalists reporting on the League of Nations Assemblies at Geneva, and on the state of post-war Europe. In both 1921 and 1933 they visited the war cemeteries on the Western Front.

Louvencourt: The small cemetery in this Somme village contains the graves of 151 Commonwealth and 76 French soldiers.

'Never Goodbye': The concluding line of a favourite poem of Roland Leighton and VB, 'Echoes: XLII' by W.E. Henley (1849–1903).

'the long white road': From the opening lines of Roland Leighton's poem 'Hédauville, November 1915'. The poem appears in TY, 226–7.

Haig: Sir Douglas (later Lord) Haig (1861–1928), British Commander-in-Chief in France, 1915–19.

Edward's Battle: The first day of the Battle of the Somme, 1 July 1916, in which Edward Brittain had led a company of the 11th Sherwood Foresters.

'Ici fut repoussé': 'Here the invasion was repelled in 1918.'

'Gaudeam adfero': 'I bring rejoicing'.

'they say the lion': From Omar Khayyam by Edward Fitzgerald (1809–83).

OTC: The Officers' Training Corps, common at public schools like Uppingham.

Frank Swinnerton: A novelist, critic and journalist (1884–1982).

Odette: Odette Keun (1888–1978), a writer, whose ten-year affair with H.G. Wells ended bitterly in 1933.

ILLUSION ON THE SOMME
New Clarion, 30 September 1933

a writer of satires on contemporary life: Winifred Holtby's *Mandoa, Mandoa!*, a comic novel about cross-race conflict and misunderstanding, and the contrast between African and European culture, had been published in 1933.

Mr Hugh Dalton: Labour politician (1887–1962). Dalton had served in France and Italy during the First World War and, like VB, became a passionate advocate of the League of Nations in the 1920s. He was later Chancellor of the Exchequer in the first Attlee Government, from 1945 to 1947.

What Would be the Character of a New War?: Published in 1931, this was a collection of essays by international experts designed to show how destructive large-scale warfare had become.

WHAT NURSING TAUGHT ME
Chelsea Hospitals Quarterly, January 1950

the tragic murder trial: VB befriended a doctor, Leonard Lockhart, after he wrote to her in 1937 about *TY*. Lockhart had been shell-shocked in France in 1918 and suffered from periodic loss of memory. In 1939, when another war looked inevitable, he killed his wife and attempted to take his own life in a kind of suicide pact. VB attended his trial, where Lockhart was found 'guilty but insane'; in 1945 she published a thinly veiled novel about Lockhart's life, called *Account Rendered*.

our present National Hospital Service: Britain's National Health Service had been established by Attlee's Labour government eighteen months earlier, in the summer of 1948.

WAR SERVICE IN PERSPECTIVE
From *Promise of Greatness. The War of 1914–1918*, edited by George A. Panichas (London: Cassell, 1968).

Kitchener's finger: The famous recruiting poster of Lord Kitchener (1850–1916), Secretary of State for War, 1914.

Arthur Ponsonby: Arthur Ponsonby (1871–1946), a leading politician and pacifist, was a Labour MP from 1922 to 1930 and Leader of the Opposition in the House of Lords 1931–35.

Rebecca West and her husband, Henry Andrews: Rebecca West (1892–1983), the writer and journalist, was married to a banker, Henry Andrews (1894–1968), who had been contemporary of Roland Leighton and Edward Brittain at Uppingham School.

the struggle for degrees for women: Oxford University granted women degrees on 7 October 1920 (VB and Winifred Holtby were among the first women in the University to matriculate). Women at Cambridge had to wait until 1948.

PHOTOGRAPH ACKNOWLEDGEMENTS

McMaster University, Hamilton, Ontario: xii, xv, xvi, xxii, 1, 2, 4, 7, 8, 13, 14, 16, 18, 19, 22, 25, 27, 28, 31, 35, 36, 42, 45, 48, 50, 54, 58, 60, 63, 64, 65, 68, 71, 72, 74, 77, 78, 81, 83, 84, 90, 94, 98, 120, 126, 133, 138, 142, 179, 195, 199, 200, 201, 209, 234.

Mark Bostridge: xxv, xxxi, 10, 32, 46, 53, 57, 97, 101, 114.

David Leighton: 40.

Imperial War Museum, London: 106, 129.

Somerville College, Oxford: 86.

Library of Congress: 102.

Outside the British cemetery at Louvencourt, where Roland Leighton
is buried. A photograph taken by Vera Brittain in 1921